Hi c

~~thous~~

I saw this book.

The

I loved trading

in my van for a car

Minivan

Best Regards

Years

Jim Gennar.

(508) 9543035

The Minivan Years

CELEBRATING THE HECTIC JOYS
OF MOTHERHOOD

Olivia Bruner

CENTER
STREET®

NEW YORK BOSTON NASHVILLE

Center Street
Hachette Book Group USA
237 Park Avenue
New York, NY 10017

Visit our Web site at www.centerstreet.com.

Center Street is a division of Hachette Book Group USA, Inc. The Center Street name and logo is a trademark of Hachette Book Group USA, Inc.

Printed in the United States of America

First Edition: January 2008

10 9 8 7 6 5 4 3 2 1

Text design by Meryl Sussman Levavi

Library of Congress Cataloging-in-Publication Data
Bruner, Olivia.
    The Minivan years : celebrating the hectic joys of motherhood / Olivia Bruner.
        p. cm.
    ISBN-13: 978-1-931722-76-6
    ISBN-10: 1-931722-76-5
    1. Child rearing. 2. Child rearing—Religious aspects. 3. Motherhood.
I. Title. II. Title: Celebrating the hectic joys of motherhood.

HQ769.B743 2008
248.8'431—dc22   2007010373

To Kyle, Shaun, Troy, and Nicole.
Thanks for being the "high" in
so many of my days.
Mom

Contents

Introduction
Welcome to the Minivan Zone   1

1 • Mini-Mishaps:
Enduring Embarrassing Times   9

2 • Mini-Morsels:
Consuming Mealtimes   19

3 • Mini-Prayers:
Requesting Miraculous Times   29

4 • Mini-Stress:
Relieving Anxious Times   39

5 • Mini-Joys:
Creating Happy Times   47

6 • Mini-Budgets:
Teaching Financial Times 57

7 • Mini-Hurts:
Redeeming Painful Times 65

8 • Mini-Sleeps:
Revitalizing Bedtimes 71

9 • Mini-Faith:
Influencing Spiritual Times 81

10 • Mini-Choices:
Deciphering Uncertain Times 91

11 • Mini-Charms:
Celebrating Feminine Times 99

12 • Mini-Sins:
Correcting Errant Times 107

13 • Mini-Enemies:
Discussing Devilish Times 117

14 • Mini-Jurisdictions:
Being-Responsible Times 125

15 • Mini-Scholars:
Choosing-a-School Times 137

16 • Mini-Heroics:
Living Sacrificial Times 147

17 • Mini-Saints:
Admiring Courageous Times 157

18 ● Mini-Perfections:
Accepting Thankful Times   165

19 ● Mini-Losses:
Grieving-Dying Times   173

Conclusion   183

About the Author   193

The
Minivan
Years

Welcome to the Minivan Zone

Not long ago I crossed a line that shoved me into a whole new dimension of motherhood: Kurt and I brought home baby number four. Adding a little princess to our assortment of budding boys meant that I finally had a child with whom I could enjoy tea parties, baby dolls, and frilly dresses. But it also meant saying good-bye to my standard automobile. Cars legally seat five, not six. And so, no matter how young, glamorous, or hip I may want to appear, I am fated to dwell in a place known as the Minivan Zone.

During college I drove a cute, yellow VW bug. Now, rear seat headphone jacks and Scotchgard are essential equipment, sporty-looking exteriors a distant fantasy.

When I was a sixth grade teacher, I wore stylish outfits to class every day. As a minivan mom, I sometimes fall into bed at night wearing the same unflattering sweats I threw on while running out the door in the morning.

As newlyweds, my husband and I enjoyed frequent candlelit dinners and passionate getaways. During the minivan years, we consider any restaurant without ketchup packets fine dining—and any bed without a child trying to wedge between us an opportunity for romantic bliss.

Whatever happened to those exhausting college years that now seem like a walk in the park, or the days when I could afford to dislike macaroni and cheese and to listen to classical music in the car instead of a Jamaican crab singing "Under the Sea" and "Kiss Da Girl"? In short, they are gone forever. And I couldn't be more grateful.

Are You in the Minivan Zone?

Whether you have four children or find yourself adjusting to your first, you know that motherhood is a lot of work. Regardless of your car size or number of children, you are in the minivan zone if

- There is at least one car seat in your vehicle—probably filled with pacifiers, cracker crumbs, smashed French fries, or M&M's.
- You spend an enormous amount of time shuttling a child among at least three extracurricular activities—including but not limited to soccer, piano lessons, and Scouts.
- Snack wrappers and Sunday school take-home papers litter the floor of your automobile.
- The best part of your day is when your youngest finally falls asleep.
- The worst part of your day is when an older sibling yells out "Mommy, come wipe me!"—waking your youngest.
- You've seen every animated feature released during the past year but can't recall finishing a single book.

It is the season when your needs go unmet and dreams seem unfulfilled. There are days of endless errands, spills, and bottles of pink antibiotic liquid. Those past this phase of motherhood remind us during the least believable moments that these are the times you will someday treasure as the best days of your life.

I suppose they're right. But why don't they seem like it? Can't we enjoy the minivan years while in them—or are we doomed to grit our teeth through what are allegedly our happiest days?

To avoid falling into that trap, I have decided to celebrate the hectic joys of motherhood today rather than wait until they are mere memories. When I am older and my children have left the nest, I want to honestly say that I enjoyed rather than endured the glory days of mommyhood. This book is my invitation for you to do likewise.

Easier Said . . .

It is much easier to say that I want to celebrate these days than actually do so. Case in point—this morning. I woke up late due to an inconsiderate alarm clock. Rushing to get the three boys fed and off to school, I remembered that Troy went to the principal's office yesterday because he wouldn't stop crying over scoring less than 100 percent on a spelling quiz. He needed to compose an apology note to his first grade teacher. While I was helping him with his fifth draft, I realized Nicole needed to wear her prettiest dress for "Mom's Morning Out" picture day. So I quickly dressed and primped her while proofing Troy's apology.

After starting the van, I went back in the house and caught Shaun watching cartoons instead of filling up his backpack—messing up the critical sequence of events needed to make it to school and my "morning out" on time. I asked my husband to watch Nicole so that I could rush the boys off to class before opening bell. When I returned, I discovered that Kurt, at Nicole's request, had removed her pretty winter dress and replaced it with a chocolate-stained summer outfit.

Then a vision of Nicole's teacher flooded my memory. "Pictures will be taken first thing," she had warned, "so everyone must be on time." We weren't.

Since today was my turn to help Shaun's teacher grade papers, I rushed home to change clothes. Days earlier my thoughtful husband had encouraged me to buy a cute blouse, probably because he is tired of the frumpy sweat-top look. I must admit, it felt good to put on something stylish for the classroom as in days of yore. That is, until I glanced in the mirror while fixing my hair to discover three stains down the front. "How did those get there?" I asked the glass with an incensed frown.

I suppose you laugh or you cry. No, it isn't easy or natural to celebrate these days. But, to be honest, I fear the alternative. Far too often we become trapped in a cycle in which frustration overwhelms happiness, anger eclipses gratitude, and resentment gradually crushes our capacity for joy. So, in the end, choosing to enjoy the minivan years may be the simpler path.

Life-giving Joy

We've all heard of the oft-quoted African American preacher who explained his reluctance to upset his wife with the line, "If Momma ain't happy, ain't nobody happy!"

Funny, but also true. My mood sets the tone in our home, for better or worse. And so does yours. When we are down in the dumps, we rob our husbands and children of the happy home they deserve. Our pity parties, lost tempers, and sulky discontent don't just drain the life out of ourselves. They set the tone for everyone under our roof.

I suppose that is why the Scriptures warn prospective husbands against women who make such attitudes a habit.

> Better to live on a corner of the roof than
> share a house with a quarrelsome wife.
>
> PROVERBS 21:9,
> NEW INTERNATIONAL VERSION (NIV)

None of us want our husbands or kids tiptoeing around the house to avoid upsetting "Momma."

Show me a woman who has learned to celebrate the hectic joys of motherhood, and I'll show you a happy home. By the same token, a woman who resents being a mommy is sowing the seeds of misery—for herself and her family.

I consider choosing happiness a moral obligation. After all, every mom has the power to be a life giver or a joy killer. I, for one, want to choose life for my family!

I invite you to join me in that pursuit as we learn together how to enjoy the sometimes hectic, sometimes exhausting blessings of living in the minivan zone. May the stories I share remind you that you are not alone and prompt the kind of smile and perspective that can inspire you to become the life-giving mother your family needs!

CHAPTER 1

Mini-Mishaps

ENDURING EMBARRASSING TIMES

I tell this story under one condition: You must promise not to report me to the child protection division of social services. It ranks among my most embarrassing moments, not to mention disqualifying me from ever writing a book on motherhood.

I would only be gone for about 210 seconds. Less than four minutes. Certainly Shaun could be trusted to watch Nicole that long.

"Shaun, you need to sit here next to the bath while I run Troy over to Kent's house." He appeared to be listening.

Nicole was then two and a half—big enough to play in a bubble bath with little risk. Kent's house was one and a half blocks away—close enough to zip there and back before anything could happen. Shaun was then ten and a half—old enough to take on such an assignment.

"Do you understand me, Shaun?" His grunt and nod told me I would be able to get Troy to his destination on time. If I took the time to get Nicole out of the bath, he would be late for soccer practice—an unpardonable parental sin.

Looking back, I realize I should have heeded that twinge of anxiety in my stomach when Shaun looked more interested in his book than my instructions. In the past, his older brother, Kyle, had taken all the keep-an-eye-on jobs. With Kyle gone, however, I had to rely on the second string.

I backed the van out of the driveway, drove the one thousand feet to Kent's house, walked Troy to Kent's door to ensure a clean handoff to Kent's mom, then zipped back home before anything could happen. Anything, that is, except what happened.

Admittedly, my zip ended up taking more than 210 seconds. Kent's mom is, like me, a chatty gal, and I've never been good at cutting off a conversation, for fear of being rude. But in this instance, I had a daughter to save from a potentially negligent son. We talked for two minutes.

As I whipped my van around the corner and approached my driveway, the world began moving in slow motion.

Passing my next-door neighbor's house, I caught a glimpse of what I could swear looked like a two-and-a-half-year-old girl standing on the front porch of Steve and Cindy Franklin's house wearing nothing but bubbles. Not good.

I parked the van and ran over to retrieve Nicole before anyone noticed, only to observe the shadow of an adult standing in Steve and Cindy's doorway. *Oh please, God, let it be Cindy!*

The next thing I remember was explaining to Steve, not Cindy, that "I instructed Shaun to keep an eye on Nicole in the bath while I zipped around the corner to take Troy . . ." You get the picture. I might even have fudged the numbers a bit, assuring Steve I had been gone only 210 seconds. As if anything I said would have wiped that *Sure, lady, I believe you!* look off his justifiably condemning face.

Steve informed me that Nicole had rung his doorbell and asked him whether her mommy was at their house because she couldn't find her at ours.

I was so angry while carrying Nicole home. At first it was aimed at my son. "How could he be so irresponsible as to walk away from the bath while a two-and-a-half-year-old girl played with her bubbles?" Then I pointed it at myself. "How could I be so stupid as to drive away from the house when a ten-year-old boy with his nose in a book grunted that he would watch my two-year-old sitting in her bubble bath?"

Every mom walking the planet has done something she regrets. Not all our mistakes can be laughed off. Something many of us know too well.

One of my close friends, Lee, pulled her car out of the garage and ran over her son Jack's scooter. A busy mother of four, she had little time to check behind the vehicle for neglected toys. She stopped the car as soon as she felt its rear end lift and drop. Wondering what she had run over, Lee pulled forward—rolling the rear tire back over the scooter in the process.

As she opened the car door to assess the damage, her worst nightmare came true. Jack, her three-year-old boy, had been riding the scooter. There he was, lying next to the rear van tire that had twice rolled over his tiny frame. Hysterically screaming her precious child's name, she slid Jack out from under the car.

I can't begin to imagine what the next several hours must have been like for Lee. A neighbor who saw what had happened called 911. Lee held her breath in hopes that the paramedics would arrive quickly; every second felt like an eternity to her. She may have killed their son.

The ambulance ride to the hospital was a blur. At the emergency room, doctors feverishly examined and x-rayed Jack's body. Friends gathered outside the emergency room as the word spread that Lee had run over Jack. Finally, everyone felt an avalanche of relief and thankfulness when the announcement was made that Jack would be fine. You see, the metal scooter that had caused the mishap also saved his life by absorbing the full weight of the car. Despite a badly bruised leg and a pretty fat lip, none of Jack's internal organs had been crushed or bones broken—even though there was a tire track halfway up his side. After being kept overnight for observation Jack walked out of the hospital the next day, went home, and got on his bike.

Even though I was mortified at the time of Nicole's bubble-bath incident, realizing something awful could have happened, I can now laugh it off. I don't recall Lee ever laughing over the scooter incident. Celebrating God's intervention? Yes. Enjoying the child she might have lost? Certainly. But laughing? Never. (Although Jack himself later teased her about the incident by asking, "Mommy, do you remember when you killed me?")

Every parent has done something he or she regrets. Others regret *not* doing something they might
have.

What parent isn't haunted by the phrase "if
only!"—the two words that inflict a daily dose of
torturous regret on millions of parents.

We regret yelling over a little bit of spilled milk
or messy bedrooms.

We regret throwing our own temper tantrums
when we should have remained calm enough to
apply the kind of loving, firm, balanced discipline
Dr. Dobson and Dr. Phil suggest.

We regret letting them eat too many sweets,
watch too much television, go to bed after nine,
and play with the unruly kids down the street.

In short, we regret being imperfect parents.

That's why I'm so glad to know that mishaps
occur even with the world's only perfect parent,
God Almighty. Of course, it wouldn't be accu-
rate to call them "mishaps" with God, since He
doesn't technically *mis* or *hap*. But bad things do
happen to God's children. And while He may not
be the cause of them, He certainly doesn't prevent them either.

Do you recall the story of the prodigal son? The
spoiled ingrate left the family farm with a wad of
cash and a negative attitude. Not exactly a parent's

dream. Sure, he eventually came home, having learned in the school of hard knocks. But not before putting his father through no small turmoil. Why didn't the father refuse to give his son the wad of cash and insist he remain in the protective sanctuary of their home? After all, good parents protect their child from mishaps—even if self-imposed. Don't they?

Of course, in the story of the prodigal son, the father represents God Himself. Like the prodigal's father, God does not try to prevent His children from making foolish choices. He grants them the freedom to decide their own course in life, even when it means squandering their entire future.

So, if a perfect parent like God encounters mishaps, I suppose you and I are in good company. More than that, I think mishaps—even when they are more than mini—serve a redemptive purpose. They push us into a place of rest we would never willingly go. The only place we can go for ultimate assurance that our children are in good hands. Not ours, His.

Every mother needs to come to the place of recognizing that her children are not, in fact, *her* children. They are God's. Sure, we have the privilege of bearing them, feeding them, comforting them, teaching them, and eventually releasing them. But we do not own them. Our overprotective impulse, while perfectly natural, is profoundly misguided. I believe God wired moms to keep kids safe so that we would nurture them toward life, not worry ourselves to death.

The apostle Paul gave valuable perspective to moms when he wrote the following.

> And we know that in all things God works for the good of those who love him, who have been called according to his purpose. . . . For I am convinced that neither death nor life, neither angels nor demons, neither the present nor the future, nor any powers, neither height nor depth, nor anything else in all creation, will be able to separate us from the love of God that is in Christ Jesus our Lord.
>
> ROMANS 8:28, 38–39, NIV

So when (not if) mishaps occur, we can rest in the knowledge that God uses all things—even imperfect moms—to accomplish His purposes in the lives of our children. Correction—*His* children.

Mini-Tip   MISHAP OFFERING

Create a list of your many motherhood mishaps from the past year. Then spend time praying over each one, asking God to forgive those that need forgiveness and use for good those that were unintentional or part of the hectic realities of life. God can redeem all things and use them in the lives of our children for good. Let God use your mishaps for a greater purpose, as He sees fit in your family.

CHAPTER 2

Mini–Morsels

CONSUMING MEALTIMES

An eight-year-long study conducted by Columbia University revealed that kids who have dinner with their parents fewer than three times a week are much more likely to smoke, drink, or use drugs than kids who have dinner with their parents five to seven times a week. Kids who dine frequently with their parents also have reduced factors of boredom, academic problems and overall stress.*

Unfortunately, the study didn't measure what all those meals together does to mom's stress level. So I thought I would shed some light on the subject.

---

*"Healthy Dining," *The Foster Letter: Religious Market Update*, Christian ministry executives newsletter, edited and published by Gary D. Foster, Van Wert, OH, July 10, 2006, p. 2.

During our B.C. era (before children) Kurt and I enjoyed dinnertime as a chance for the two of us to set aside the demands of our respective careers and devote all our attention to each other. Even a quick sandwich with chips served to calm our chaos and allowed us to look into each other's eyes as we enjoyed two of life's great pleasures—dining and conversation. After the meal, we spent even more time cleaning up our dishes together.

After God added children to our table, mealtime became an entirely different experience. We still occasionally go to a restaurant, but candles have been replaced by ketchup packets. Rather than the time of day I anticipated as a chance to relax with my husband, mealtime became the hour during which Kurt and I would most likely have nervous breakdowns. I had to plan and prepare the meal, inevitably send Kurt to the store in the middle of preparation to get that missing ingredient, set the table, and then corral the kids. Once we got the food and family to the table, the real drama began.

DAD: Whose turn is it to say the blessing tonight?
NICOLE: I'll pray!
MOM: Nicole, you've prayed every night for the past two years. I think it might be one of your brothers' turn.

NICOLE: But I want to pray!

DAD: Okay. First Kyle will pray and then Nicole can pray.

Every night we made the same compromise. So every night the food cooled while we waited for Nicole to thank God for every imaginable blessing—from her most recent toy to her playtime with friends to the lovely sky to each member of the family. Very sweet, but hunger pangs do call.

"Amen!" Dad gently interrupts five minutes into Nicole's prayer.

I jump up to zap the serving dishes in the microwave and return to the table with hot food. In our B.C. years, I warmed up leftovers. Now I warm up meals before the first bite.

As soon as we begin passing the food around, the countdown begins. Within five minutes, at most eight, someone will invariably knock over his or her drink. As the law of gravity assures that heavy objects will fall downward, the law of mealtime assures that kid elbows will catch cups. Sure, I warn the children to keep their drinks away from the edge. Sure, they slide them toward the middle of the table. But preventative measures are futile. The cups will end up back on the edge after their next sips.

Like a crowd doing the wave at the baseball stadium, every member of the family jumps up from the table with hands raised in reaction to the splash. I quickly take charge, ordering the little ones away from the mess and the older boys to start clearing. Kurt typically rushes to grab a towel, right after angrily calling down judgment on the child whose elbow created the mess.

I'm convinced whoever coined the phrase "No use crying over spilled milk" never had kids. For I used to cry—or at least yell. But I learned that it only makes matters worse. Besides, after the five hundredth spill you get used to it.

Confident the spill quota has been filled for the evening, we restore the table to order and again heat the food so we can carry on with our meal. We work through the rest of our routine, including our favorite mealtime activity, which Kurt triggers with the phrase "high low!"

"High low!" means the time has come for each person to share the high point of his day and the low point of his day. I might share, for example, that my high point came when Troy wrote me a little note of encouragement—while my low point came when Troy's elbow hit the cup.

Kurt, on the other hand, might share that his high point came when he kissed Mommy upon arriving home from work—while his low point came when Mommy didn't name it as her high point.

Kyle might share a high test score as his high and showing up late for band practice as his low.

Troy's high typically involves some sporting activity, such as a roller hockey goal or beating Dad playing HORSE in basketball. His low, on the other hand, probably came when he missed a shot or lost to Dad.

Nicole doesn't quite get the point of the activity, since she typically lists everything she enjoyed doing the preceding two months. She loves life and has a hard time limiting her celebrations to a single day.

Our high-low routine took on special significance during Shaun's fourth-grade year. I remember the evening he skipped naming a high and went immediately to his low. Suddenly, mealtime became more than a chance to feed the family and overwork the microwave. It opened the door to uncovering some deep hurts in our second child's life. My heart sank when I learned his friends had turned against him at school. But it enabled us to intervene. Before long, Shaun's sagging head returned to its former confidence position. If it hadn't been for our mealtime routine, however, I fear we might not have learned about the problem until more damage had been done.

Other mealtimes brought on other kid challenges. It was during a postspill conversation that we learned of Kyle's debate with a biased science teacher, opening the door for Kurt to help him defend the intellectual rigor of Christian belief. We discovered and corrected Troy's disrespectful attitude toward a teacher after he listed getting in trouble at school as the day's low. And we found out Nicole hadn't been as nice as the preschool director implied when it came to sharing. All thanks to a little routine called high low.

I think I understand why kids who eat meals with their parents five to seven nights a week do better. Despite the stress it adds to my life and the mess it creates on my table, I think the time and energy invested pay handsome dividends in the lives of four very important people.

In addition to strategies like high low to discover what is going on in your children's lives, I'd like to suggest several approaches for instilling values and beliefs into your child's mind and heart. Try some of these to turn mealtime into one of the most meaningful, spiritually rich parts of your family life.

DINNER TABLE DEBATE

A great way to help our children better grasp and defend what they believe is to create dinner table debate discussions. Choose the day you plan to hold your debate during dinner and assign different sides of the issue to individuals or teams. (For example, Mom and son take one side of a topic while Dad and daughter take the opposite side.) Give the teams several days or weeks to prepare for the debate. When the big day arrives, remind everyone to bring his or her notes and be prepared to begin the debate immediately after eating. It is wise to assign a moderator or clearly establish rules for the debate in order to keep everything fair and under control.

If you choose to have dinner table debates in your home, consider several important points. First, you may be concerned about seriously entertaining arguments that oppose your beliefs. However, it is better for your children to struggle with these issues in the safety and spirit of a believing family than wait until they are exposed to these ideas in a less supportive context. Second, this requires some work on the part of the parents. You must be willing to learn along with your kids—including taking the time to read and prepare. It may do more harm than good to organize a debate in which you can't engage. Ask your youth pastor to recommend some helpful resources.

"WHAT IF" DISCUSSION

Use "what if" questions to help your children think through important truths. For example, help your kids appreciate the implications of a Christian view of personal worth by contrasting it with other belief systems. Schedule a dinner table discussion in which you pose the following "what if" scenarios:

Question: What if Mom and Dad (or God) only loved and accepted the person in the family who was the best at playing marbles?
Answer: Most of us would be unhappy and spend all our time trying to become marbles experts.

Question: What if those who became slave traders had believed that all people have personal worth?
Answer: They would have opposed rather than promoted slavery.

Question: What if the Founding Fathers had believed Darwin's theory that only the fit will survive?
Answer: They would never have written our Constitution on the idea that "all men are created equal. . . ."

Question: What if Adolf Hitler had believed that all people deserved respect because they are created in the image of God?

Answer: There might never have been the Holocaust.

The possible topics and questions are endless, providing another way to make mealtime conversations meaningful to your children.

THE JOB INTERVIEW

Set aside one dinnertime discussion session to have your children place themselves in the shoes of an employer who is looking for a good worker. Create a list of different careers and jobs, and for each one, ask your children to describe what qualities they would want in the person they want to hire. Keep a list of similar themes that should emerge with every role—such as working hard; being on time, friendly, obedient; etc. You may even want to role-play with the children by pretending to be a job applicant and answering questions they create for you. Use this discussion to reinforce the qualities we should strive to build into our own lives.

The next time you find yourself cleaning up a dinner table spill, instead of becoming angry, use it as a reminder of just how important mealtime conversation can be. The mini-morsels you and your children receive from intentional conversation might just become the tastiest part of your day.

Mini-Tip　　　HIGH AND LOW

Begin the habit of going around the dinner table and asking each person to take turns sharing his or her high and low for that day. When you proclaim high low, everyone will know it is his or her opportunity to be open with the family about the best and worst moments of the day. You will be amazed to learn what your child considers the highlight—perhaps something small that gives insight into what brings him joy. You will also discover painful moments you might not have otherwise known—providing an opportunity to comfort, encourage, intervene, or do whatever might be appropriate.

CHAPTER 3

Mini-Prayers

REQUESTING MIRACULOUS TIMES

I'd like to think of myself as a woman of prayer. But then, I'd also like to think of myself as a size four. Motherhood, with its hectic schedules and leftover baby weight, seems to have placed both out of reach.

The real prayer warrior in our family turns out to be Troy. At eight, he is too old to merely parrot *"God is good, God is great"* prayer poems, yet young enough to still take seriously Jesus' invitation to "ask, and it will be given to you."

I offer as evidence our 2006 trip to attend Kurt's family reunion. We awoke early that morning in order to finalize packing and get to the airport on time. Since the Denver airport was about a ninety-minute drive from our house, we planned a "no later than 10 A.M." departure to catch our 12:30 flight. But something went wrong in the space-time continuum that day.

While casually pulling out of the garage to hit the ATM before stopping off at the library on our way to the freeway, both Kurt and I noticed the clock mocking us by displaying 10:30 A.M.—a full thirty minutes beyond our no-later-than limit. Each assuming the other had been time monitor, we simultaneously glared at each other with identical looks: *You realize there is no way in the world we are going to make it in time to check our luggage, get all six of us through security, and make our plane before departure—and it is your fault.*

Moments later, we found ourselves speeding past the ATM and library toward the freeway, Kurt shouting near obscenities while I dialed the airline on my cell phone to find out whether the plane might be mercifully delayed.

Fifteen minutes and two hundred automated agent questions later, I finally reached a live person who checked our flight status. She perkily responded by informing me: "We are proud to say that we project yet another on-time departure." Great.

Fearing a mad rush up the freeway would be both dangerous and futile, I suggested to Kurt that

we give up and book ourselves on the 5 P.M. flight—
a prospect neither of us favored, since we had a
six-hour drive ahead of us after reaching Chicago.
While the two of us shouted pros and cons of our
options as if weapons in the unspoken *You got us
into this mess!* blame game, Troy spoke up from the
backseat. "We could pray."

Silence overtook the grown-ups arguing up front.

"We could ask God to help us get to the airport
on time and safe so that we make the flight," Troy
continued.

After a brief pause to regain his composure and slip
into a more spiritual tone, Kurt responded, "That's a
good idea, Troy. Will you lead us in prayer?"

"Dear God. Please keep us safe and help us make
it to the plane on time. In Jesus' name. Amen."
Simple and to the point. Not to mention infinitely
more appropriate than Mom or Dad's behavior.

Having evaporated the tension in the van air,
our youngest asked if she, too, could pray—which
she did.

Our faith was less than strong, but we continued driving. I suppose we were a bit like Peter who
took a few steps on the water before sinking. He
wanted to believe but saw the ominous waves.
We wanted to believe, but saw 11:08 A.M. on the
clock with forty-five miles to go.

Don't ask me how, but we made it to the airport precisely one hour before the scheduled departure time. Call it a mini-miracle. Call it bending the speed limit laws. Call it what you will. All I know is that Kurt dropped me and the kids at the counter in time to check in our bags. As he sped away from the curb to find what ended up being the last open parking spot on the premises, the rest of us looked down at our little prayer warrior, who was grinning from ear to ear.

Other opportunities for Troy to remind us of Jesus' invitation to prayer emerged on that same trip. Like the time we accidentally left the backpack containing our camera on the Chicago train requiring "miraculous" retrieval, then doing it again exiting a departing city bus, and another mad rush to the airport trying to return our rental van on time. All of them silly little incidents. But none too insignificant for a Troy-inspired prayer.

Only a few weeks before that family reunion trip another prayer aimed at saving our daughter's life. Nicole and Troy were playing with a pile of LEGOs in the bedroom. Kurt, reading in our room, jumped from his chair when he heard a panicked yell from Troy.

"Nicole! Oh no! Oh no!" Troy screamed.

Clearly something bad had occurred, much

worse than a typical childhood mishap. Kurt rushed into the hallway, where he saw Troy jumping up and down while clasping his hands in a posture of desperate prayer.

"What happened?" shouted Kurt as he looked at Nicole on the floor just outside the bedroom door.

"It's in her throat. She can't breathe!"

As Kurt approached a crouching Nicole and tried to process Troy's statement, our precious little girl coughed up a small plastic ball. She had been sucking it and had accidentally swallowed it. It had lodged in her windpipe and prevented air from getting in or out.

I arrived home from the store about thirty minutes later. As I listened to Kurt explain what happened, tears filled my eyes at the realization of how close we had come to tragedy. I hugged her and hugged her and hugged her some more. I then glanced over at Troy, my little prayer warrior, who was grinning from ear to ear.

To say that prayer is important is a bit like saying the sky is up. Who would ever argue? But, in truth, I sometimes find myself wondering what, exactly, prayer does.

I participate in a ministry called Moms in Touch. Every Wednesday morning after dropping the kids off at school, I join a group of mothers who gather at a designated house near the high school campus in order to pray for their children. Unlike at our small-group gatherings at church, there is no food served or chitchat about this and that. We start at 8:30 A.M. and by 8:35 A.M. get down to the business of prayer for anything and everything related to our children at school. We pray that the Lord will keep our kids safe. We pray over fifth period math exams. We even pray for the teachers and school administrators.

One day our group learned that a boy had been arrested at my son's high school after it was discovered that he had a gun in his locker. Immediately visions of Eric Harris and Dylan Klebold shooting their classmates at Columbine High years earlier came into our minds. We breathed a collective sigh of relief that the gun had been discovered. But we also worried that such an unthinkable possibility had entered our zip code.

"We should give thanks." One of our in-touch moms shared from her heart before we began praying. "We've been praying that God would protect our kids. He has answered that prayer!"

Who can argue with that? And yet, I can't get away from certain questions.

I recall sitting on a plane next to a sweet old lady who told me the story of her granddaughter.

Despite a thriving Moms in Touch ministry among the parents of Columbine High, her granddaughter nearly died in that shooting spree. The girl's best friend did die after answering "yes" to the "Do you believe in God?" question. While the lady's grand-daughter survived, removing the shrapnel from her body has left terrible scars and required removing one of her virgin breasts—with the other still vulnerable to lingering infections.

Did God protect her, thanks to the prayers of the Columbine Moms in Touch group? Or did God overrule their petition in favor of some mysterious higher purpose?

I guess we can't know the answer.

Someone has said that prayer is the greatest act of faith because, unlike church attendance or charitable giving or Bible reading where other people and things provide tangible reinforcement, prayer is just you talking to someone you can't see about matters you hope He cares to hear.

Troy is pretty confident that God listens and cares. Troy takes Jesus at His word when he invited us to "Ask and it will be given to you." But the rest of that invitation causes one to wonder . . .

> Which of you, if his son asks for bread,
> will give him a stone? Or if he asks for a

fish, will give him a snake? If you, then, though you are evil, know how to give good gifts to your children, how much more will your Father in heaven give good gifts to those who ask him!

MATTHEW 7:9–12, NIV

High school students getting shot rather than being kept safe feels like a snake rather than a fish to me.

Why is it our Moms in Touch group could give thanks for a gun found in time, while the Columbine group attended funerals?

"Ye have not," the King James Bible proclaimed "because ye ask not."

Well, maybe we ask not because He sometimes gives not. I often ask but add "if it be your will," to give God an escape clause. After all, Jesus taught the disciples to pray by telling them to add, "Thy Kingdom come, Thy will be done." That's pretty safe. But I somehow doubt passively telling God to "do whatever You think best" is what He had in mind.

So how do I approach praying for my kids? Do I, like Troy, go boldly before the throne of grace and list all my concerns, requests, and hopes, confident He listens and cares? In short, yes. How do I know? Because of the opening words of the prayer Jesus used to teach us how to pray: "Our Father."

Every father—or mother, for that matter—wants his child to ask for things. When we can, we like to say yes to those requests. When we think it a harmful request, we say no. When we find it impossible to accommodate the request, we say no. The request itself, however, is a vital part of the child-parent relationship. Children ask. Parents decide and respond. If the two have a trusting relationship, the child recognizes the parent will do what he or she believes best. Even if that means hearing the word no.

So what about Columbine and other such "snakes" that force their way into the lives of God's children? Why does God allow such things? That, I must confess, remains a mystery.

So, as God's daughter, I ask. But I do so in a spirit of humility, recognizing that He is God, and I am not. Or should I say, He is the parent, and I the child.

For now, I give thanks. For a safe high school. For a toy ball popping out of my daughter's throat. For making it to the airport on time. And for a son who has far more faith than his mommy.

Mini-Tip   SAYING THANKS

Our children see us pray over meals, pray before bed, and pray while trying to catch a plane, but we rarely highlight the times those prayers are answered. So, next time you sit down for a meal with your children, ask everyone to mention some answer to prayer your family has received. Nothing is too small. The food you are about to eat, for example, can be celebrated as God's answer to "Give us this day our daily bread" prayed in church on Sunday. Even thank God for saying no to things that we might not understand but that we trust He will use for good.

CHAPTER 4

Mini-Stress

RELIEVING ANXIOUS TIMES

Mommy, I think this is the happiest vacation we've ever had."

We all go through stressful seasons in life. The years leading up to Troy's "happiest vacation" declaration still qualify as our harshest winter. Kurt had taken on a new, gigantic responsibility during a period of transition at Focus on the Family, so he was good for little around the house. Kyle and Shaun decided to enter early adolescence, complete with body-odor-generating, remembering-homework-evaporating, bad-attitude-spawning testosterone tidal waves. In addition, we had recently buried my mom after her prolonged battle with Parkinson's disease—ending a five-year period in which

I transitioned from my mother's daughter to my mother's mom. I'm certain that we would have fallen into the bright-red danger zone had we had time to take a stress-o-meter test.

"You know," Troy continued, "we don't have any stron—any stran—any— Oh, what is that word, Mommy?"

"Do you mean stress?" I interpreted.

"Yeah, *stress*! That's the word."

I hadn't thought about how our harsh winter might have affected Troy. At seven years old, I assumed him blissfully immune. I guess we overlook the dangers of secondhand anxiety. *Such a sweet boy*, I thought, picking up clues to how his mom and dad must feel and expressing how happy he is that we had a few weeks to relax. He was generally submerged in his own world of activities, and I hadn't realized he had it in him to be so sensitive.

"Like for me," he continued, "when we are at home I have to worry about what time my next hockey practice will be."

As it turned out, he didn't have it in him. Mom or Dad's stress hadn't even crossed his mind.

On the one hand, it makes a mom feel good that her son can skate happily from one hockey practice to the next with only a vague awareness of the stress we grown-ups endure. On the other hand, what need does he have to "worry about what I'm going to do next" in his life when I have such matters well in hand—safely entered into my PDA so that it will beep on cue to make sure we arrive at the right place at the right time?

He doesn't need to worry. But he worries, nonetheless. As do the rest of my kids.

Kyle stresses over retaining first chair trombone in the band because the girl he took it from is determined to get it back.

Shaun worries that our dog might dart out the front door and get lost in the wilds of our suburban housing development.

Nicole invests tremendous emotional energy into picking the right dress for her play date at fellow five-year-old Ellie's house. She knows she's a princess in Daddy's eyes at home. But entering the princess-eat-princess world of make-believe at a friend's house is a whole different matter. One can't be too particular about wardrobe. "She won't think I'm beautiful!" comes the objection if I try to grab something quick and easy to throw on her.

And then there's Troy, who, we've already established, worries about getting to his next hockey practice on time.

I don't remember ever teaching my kids how to feel stress, so I guess anxiety is part of the human condition. There isn't much I can do about the blizzard of troublesome burdens that swirl around our lives outside the walls of my house and minivan. But I can do my best to create a refuge from the storm.

When our second boy, Shaun, was in the fourth grade, he endured a season of prolonged stress thanks to Paul, the class bully who chose him as his annual extracurricular project. Most of the other kids had been intimidated into joining his gang. By the middle of the year, Shaun remained the lone holdout. As a result, he became the target of verbal abuse. You know the routine. In gym class, Shaun always got picked last. At recess, he had no one to play with. At lunch, he endured snide comments. In short, he hated going to school. Kurt and I intervened on several occasions, demanding that the teacher and principal step in. But Paul's mom was part of the school office staff and sided with her son, so nothing really changed.

I remember watching Shaun walk through our front door after enduring another stress-filled day at school and seeing his downcast demeanor lift—like he had just slipped into a warm bath after playing in the freezing snow. You see, when Shaun entered our home he knew he had a refuge, a place where he would be affirmed rather than attacked, respected rather than ridiculed, enjoyed rather than ignored. We eventually pulled Shaun out of class and I schooled him at home for a few years—but not before learning an important lesson about the anchor a loving family provides to a turbulent life.

If someone had placed a stress-o-meter inside my home as I was growing up, they would have seen the environment as anything but a refuge. The last place I wanted to be as a young girl was at my house. I came up with every excuse possible to play at a friend's house, eat at a friend's house, even spend the night at a friend's house—often without informing my mom I would be gone. Not that she noticed. A single mom, her life was too chaotic to keep track of all six kids. And since I rarely gave her trouble, she invested little energy worrying about what I did or where I went. She had much bigger worries on her mind. Namely, my four older brothers. One was deaf, requiring special schooling and attention—neither of which my mom could really afford to give. The others experienced all sorts of problems related to having an abusive or absent dad.

No wonder neighborhood parents warned their kids to avoid our house. Like I said, it was the last place even I wanted to be. So I didn't try to tell anyone of the stresses I experienced at school or with friends. Even if I did, no one would have heard over all the shouting.

I hate to think of what my life might have become. But by God's grace I found a substitute refuge. My best friend during my adolescence was Darcie. Her dad, Randy, pastored a little Baptist church in our neighborhood. The congregation never grew much. A thoughtful teacher more than a charismatic preacher, Randy couldn't attract big crowds like many of his colleagues. He might have felt like a failure, but to me he couldn't have been a greater success. You see, he loved his wife and children. He created a stable home where the family ate meals together, talked about problems, laughed together, and enjoyed one another's company. The kind of family I longed to have myself. I thank God every day that the Piersma family allowed an ill-kept, needy girl like me to hang out with them. And I thank Randy for putting his fatherly arms around a hurting adolescent to show me what a father should be—and what a family could be.

Every child needs a refuge from the inevitable anxieties of life—especially during the minivan years when what might seem a small concern to you feels like an enormous burden to them.

I know what you're thinking: *But I can hardly*

*handle the stress of my own concerns, much bigger mat-
ters than the petty issues my kids endure!*

I hear you. As you'll recall, I started this chapter surprised that my seven-year-old worries about
things like getting to hockey practice on time. It
never occurred to me since he doesn't have to pay
a mortgage, manage six schedules, cook and clean,
organize car pools, color his hair to hide the gray, or
care for a dying mom. From where I sit, his mini-
anxieties don't even compare to my maxi-stress!

But then I remember the obvious. God invites
me to take refuge in Him so that I'll have the ability
to create a refuge for others.

> Cast all your anxiety on him because he
> cares for you.
>
> I Peter 5:7, NIV

You see, from where God sits, your biggest concern
is a mere mini-stress. So you, like Troy, have no
need to worry.

> Therefore I tell you, do not worry about
> your life, what you will eat or drink; or
> about your body, what you will wear. Is not
> life more important than food, and the body
> more important than clothes? . . . [Do] not

worry about tomorrow, for tomorrow will
worry about itself.

MATTHEW 6:25–26, 34, NIV

So until tomorrow, why not take a break from
your mini-stress so that you can give your child,
and maybe some needy neighborhood kid, a refuge
from theirs.

Mini-Tip   START TIME

As soon as your children begin sleeping through the night,
get in the habit of setting your alarm clock at least thirty
minutes before they tend to wake in order to mentally
prepare yourself for the day ahead. You can review your
day's schedule and goals and perhaps even have a time
for prayer and Bible reading. This may sound ludicrous
since motherhood is so exhausting that we want to put off
crawling out of bed until the last possible moment. But,
remember, motherhood is our job. When I was a teacher
starting my classroom duties at 8 A.M., I always got up at
least an hour before then to shower and get ready. Waking up to the immediate demands of your "job" as a mom
adds stress far more exhausting than what is gained by
thirty minutes more of shut-eye.

CHAPTER 5

Mini-Joys

CREATING HAPPY TIMES

We roll along in the van, approaching the Disneyland gate. Everyone feels excited and a bit anxious. Kyle and Shaun, our older boys, see Thunder Mountain. Their stomachs tense with the knowledge that this year both are old enough to ride.

At four, Troy feels nervous about running into Mickey or some other character. He knows they walk around the park greeting children, a prospect that has given him nightmares. It is one thing to enjoy their shenanigans on-screen, but to come face-to-face with a giant Goofy? Scary! "Don't worry, Troy," we reassure him. "We'll tell them to stay away from you."

Nicole is eighteen months, but even she feels the excitement in the air.

We reach the parking attendant, and Kurt pulls out his wallet to fork over the first of many bills to be spent this day—the start of his anxiety. Meanwhile, I begin giving instructions to the children. I know what to expect and want to head off problems at the pass.

To Troy: "Remember, some of the lines will be long, so you'll need to be patient."

To the older boys: "We'll be going back and forth between big kid and little kid rides, so no complaining."

To everyone: "You can each have one sweet snack, so choose wisely."

And most important of all: "I don't want to hear any whining today."

Yeah, *right*! As if that one ever works. Still, warning children helps to minimize offenses. Or so we like to believe.

The day goes pretty much as you might expect. Lots of fun mixed with impatient line waiting, complaints about the kiddy rides, incessant whining, and too many sweets.

Disneyland calls itself "the happiest place on earth." That's its goal. That's its image. Just watch the commercials—always a cute, balloon-holding happy toddler hugging Mickey Mouse on Main Street. You never see a hot, whining four-year-old running for his life from Goofy.

Still, Disneyland does pretty well living up to its motto. But I am convinced that it is not so much going to Disneyland that creates happiness, as much as the anticipation leading up to Disneyland and the memories that come after.

The weeks approaching our Disneyland trip? Terrific. Kids on their best behavior in response to Dad's empty threats to cancel the trip if chores weren't done and attitudes checked. Nighttime dreams filled with the sights, sounds, and smells of the Magic Kingdom. Daytime conversation packed with attraction descriptions and character imitations. It seems that the longer we looked forward to the day, the more happiness we squeezed out of the experience.

And the weeks, months, and years following the trip? Also great. Our camcorder tape and photos remind us of the fun. Our memory banks recall the best moments of the day and seem to edit out the bad scenes (or enable us to finally laugh at them). Troy forgets his panic. I forget the whining. Even Kurt forgets the cost. Looking back, we all see it as a perfect day.

It's often that way in life. The file cabinet of our

minds places happy memories and fond reflections on top and in front, while hiding the unpleasant ones in a remote bottom drawer. Sure, we can find them if absolutely necessary. But who wants to?

While enduring the torture of labor pains, I wondered why I ever allowed Kurt to touch me. Five minutes after giving birth, however, I knew only the joyful tears of welcoming a new life.

I fondly remember the moment I walked across the stage to receive my college degree. I forget about the boring lectures, textbooks, and term paper deadlines.

It would be just as easy to remember only the bad; many people choose to do that. But the deeper desire for happiness overtakes my memories of frustration, regret, and pessimism. Why is that? Does the tendency to remember happy times and forget frustration suggest emotional health or mental illness? I suppose it depends upon whether you believe we were made to smile or made to frown.

It is difficult to pinpoint the exact moment happiness occurs. In fact, I'm not sure we can. We experience happiness—like love or gratitude—apart from a particular time or place. Circumstance neither triggers nor constrains it. It is more spiritual than emotional. And like the best gifts, it often arrives when least expected.

I think we desire happiness because we feel homesick. We were made to be happy because we were made to know God. When we encounter happiness, however brief, we catch a glimpse of someone we have never seen but miss nonetheless. Nothing can change the simple reality that we long for joy. We long to go home. Circumstances cannot steal from the truly happy or give to the truly miserable. Neither depends upon their proximity to pleasure, health, or money. They depend, rather, upon their proximity to God.

Of course, it would be silly to suggest that only those with faith experience happiness. I've met too many happy unbelievers to think that. Moments of joy, like drops of rain, will fall on the believer and the atheist alike. But the refreshment of water and the lift of a smile have the same source. Without God, crops die and faces frown.

Smiles provide much-needed reminders that we were made for happiness, like sips of a drink we long to guzzle. Sure, they fall far short of the reality we desire. But they won't let us forget that we were made for something more. Something even better than Disneyland.

Have you ever known one of those couples who have been blessed with terrific kids? You know the ones. They are the family you watch from afar, wondering how in the world they got so lucky or did so well. It is almost as if they have discovered a secret formula for raising great kids.

We have been fortunate over the years to build relationships with some of those couples, watching over the long haul as they navigate the varied and perilous stages of parenthood. Their children have grown from little kids to young adults, and though imperfect, have turned out quite well. Many of them are approaching the end of the parenting journey and are reaping the rewards of having done some things right. Let us give you a peek into what we've learned from these little-known, greatly respected examples of parental success.

In the last chapter I mentioned the Piersmas, who were a major influence on my life when I was a teenager and young adult. In their house—unlike in mine—Dad, Mom, and the kids actually seemed to enjoy one another. They loved unconditionally. They talked over dinner and seemed to care about what the others were saying. They laughed together, played together, teased together, even took vacations together. Through the good and bad, they liked being together. Their enjoyment was almost contagious.

Decades later, the Piersmas still enjoy one another. They've been separated by distance as the kids have left home to start families of their own. Several of the children have gone through some serious struggles. Still, the close ties established early remain strong. We can't help but wonder, when so many families struggle just to survive, what "secret formula" helped the Piersma family thrive.

Then there are the Ledbetters. We have watched this family in action for nearly twenty years, and we have come to admire and covet the success they've experienced in the parenting process. With two grown children and a teenager at home, Otis and Gail Ledbetter are beginning to enjoy a return on their parenting efforts. All three kids consider Mom and Dad to be among their best friends; all three have adopted Mom and Dad's values. Certainly, they have their own opinions and preferences, but the apples have remained pretty close to the tree. Why, when so many kids are rejecting the faith and values of their parents, did the Ledbetter children readily embrace theirs? What is their "secret formula"?

If you ask Mike and Terri Beidermann to tell you about their four teenagers, be prepared for an extensive bragging session. They are proud of their kids, as they should be. Though by no means perfect, the Beidermann children reflect the love and investment of diligent, intentional parents. They have good morals, manners, discipline, and a good amount of success. They also have questions, struggles, failures, and a healthy dose of uncertainty about what they believe. But they continue to believe. They embrace the faith and values modeled by Mom and Dad even when it is unpopular to do so. Once again, the "secret formula" has worked wonders.

What is this "secret formula" for successfully passing our values to the next generation? What is the common thread among these and other families who seem to have beaten the odds in the parenting process? As we've watched over the years, we have seen the same important ingredient. The specific tone and makeup of each family varies, but the "secret formula" is the same. Every one of these couples discovered and mastered the art of enjoying their children and of allowing their children to enjoy them. Put simply—they learned to create an environment where they had fun together!

Observing the Piersmas, the Ledbetters, the Beidermanns, and other families has convinced us that laugher and fun are incredibly powerful tools in the process of passing values. While much of this book is dedicated to giving principles and ideas on how to teach our kids, it assumes a context of enjoying our kids. That, we believe, is one of the most important ingredients for increasing the odds.

When Kurt spends time wrestling with our boys in the basement, he does more to make our values stick than when he reads them a Bible passage. Both are important, but the former makes the latter more meaningful.

When I play a round of Go Fish with Shaun, he learns to enjoy me as a person, not merely obey me as a parent and authority figure. Again, both are important, but the former makes the latter easier to accept.

Everyone has the right to speak, but one must earn the right to be listened to. As parents, we must realize that when we play with our kids today, we are earning the right to shape their values tomorrow. Remember, they are more likely to embrace the values of someone they love and enjoy than of someone they don't. So let's adopt the secret formula that seems to have worked so well for so many parents. Let's have fun with our kids!

Mini-Tip   FUN DAY

If you lack the creativity or inclination for spontaneous fun, go ahead and force the issue by placing "Fun Day" on the weekly calendar to make sure you intentionally plan something the kids will enjoy. It could be as simple as making chocolate chip pancakes for Saturday morning breakfast, getting out the Junior Monopoly game when they come home from school, or scheduling a picnic dinner on the living room floor. Just ask the kids for a list of suggestions, and fill the calendar with joy!

CHAPTER 6

Mini-Budgets

TEACHING FINANCIAL TIMES

When preparing for a vacation, we moms worry about packing enough socks, underwear, toiletries, and clothes. The kids, on the other hand, worry about the really important stuff—like swimsuits, stuffed animals, and coloring books. On our most recent trip, then five-year-old Nicole became particularly intense about bringing a small, pink pocket purse she had been using to store her personal Fort Knox—a collection of coins assembled over the preceding months by snatching up every bit of loose change she could find.

Some of the quarters, dimes, nickels, and pennies had been found on counters and nightstands. But most had come from Daddy's pocket.

Mastering the fine art of feminine persuasion at an early age, Nicole discovered the secret to sudden wealth—puppy dog eyes behind periodic "Daddy, can I have some money?" inquiries. Her recent take: two dollars and fifty-seven cents, not including the random coins that brought the total beyond the three-dollar threshold.

Now comes the really impressive part. Nicole managed to go two whole vacation days carrying that purse around without spending a single penny. She protected her stash in anticipation of day three, when the family would visit Greenfield Village and the Henry Ford Museum where she would see horse-drawn carriages, ride a historic train, and, above all, visit the gift shop filled with wonderfully useless souvenirs. Useless souvenirs that would of course require a significant portion of her net worth.

Before we even set foot inside the park, Nicole's gaze fixed upon the most amazing contraption her young eyes had ever beheld—one of those machines that takes an ordinary penny and smashes it into a smooth, flat keepsake and imprints a picture of an early Ford automobile. Of course, the privilege of turning your penny into a worthless trinket cost fifty cents—bringing the total investment up to just over half a dollar. What's worse, it required removing from the purse two quarters—bringing her supply of coins down from eight to six. After a momentary hesitation, however, she decided it was a worthy way to spend part of her vast fortune.

After placing the flat copper thingy inside her purse in place of the fifty-one cents, Nicole moved on to enjoy the park—still anticipating that wonderful moment at the end of the day when the entire family would walk into the gift shop to watch her choose any souvenir her heart desired.

Two hours and thirty-seven minutes later, Nicole encountered yet another wonder. This time, a machine that formed hot plastic into one of two shapes: a Model T Ford or a bust of Henry Ford himself. No five-year-old could live without one of those. So, against Mom's urging to save her money, Nicole chose the bust—eagerly retrieving eight shiny quarters to slip into the money slot before pressing the magic button that turned ten cents' worth of plastic into a keepsake certain to be discarded before day's end.

Moments later as the thrill of retrieving her very own Henry Ford subsided, Nicole opened her purse to assess the damage. "Buyer's remorse" doesn't begin to describe her reaction.

"Ohhhhhhh noooooo!" came a high-pitched whine.

"What's the matter?" I inquired, assuming she might have discovered a flaw on Henry's likeness. I noticed her peering into her pink purse with an angry scowl, as if some thief had stolen her prized possession. Peering over Nicole's slumping shoulders, I glanced into the purse. Where there had previously been a supply of large, shiny quarters now sat a pitiful pile of pennies, nickels, and a dime or two. Her Fort Knox had become a pauper's box.

"I didn't want to spend my money on that!" a weeping Nicole exclaimed.

Teachable moments just don't come more perfectly wrapped. I seized the opportunity and with the most compassionate voice I could muster said, "Well, Nicole, you've learned a good lesson through this. You have to be careful with your money, saving it for what is really important."

Nicole immediately stopped crying, a puzzled look overtaking her face. She looked up at me with indignant condescension and corrected a statement that, from her perspective, had nothing whatsoever to do with her present distress.

"I didn't learn that lesson, Mommy!" she corrected. "I learned that I need more money!"

Tell me about it, sweetheart. Tell me about it!

Years before Nicole or Troy came along, Kurt and I conducted a little exercise with our older boys to teach them the value of money. Viewing an allowance as a good way to help kids learn to budget, we decided to start giving then eight-year-old Kyle and six-year-old Shaun a few dollars per week to manage. Before doing so, however, we wanted to teach them the basic biblical principles of financial stewardship.

We scheduled a family night to create an object lesson that the boys would never forget. Kurt went to the bank and withdrew one thousand one-dollar bills. After receiving some odd looks from the bank teller, she complied and handed over a big chunk of our life savings. Cash in hand, we were ready for the big event.

To start our family night we told the boys that we had hidden a treasure somewhere in the house for them to find. They excitedly began their search, running from one room to the next looking for who knows what. Before long, we heard Shaun scream out in disbelief. He had found the money pile.

We caught up with the boys downstairs, right

where we expected. What we didn't expect, however, was such an enthusiastic reaction. Both of them were throwing money in the air, rolling about in an ocean of cash as Shaun exclaimed, "We're rich! We're rich! Now we can buy a house with a swimming pool and a Nintendo Sixty-Four!"

"Just a minute." Dad's wet blanket landed with a plop. "Before going too crazy, we need to follow God's instructions for money." The boys gave each other a knowing glance. As suspected, a lesson had to be learned before the fun could begin.

"Once we follow God's instructions for money, we are going to let you guys spend the money on whatever you want!" Kurt explained, rekindling their anticipation. "Look through the pile and find an envelope labeled God's Instructions for Money so we can get started."

The envelope contained a letter detailing several steps the children had to follow in order to discover biblical guidelines for finances. To start, they had to count the cash. We had no idea just how long it would take for an eight- and six-year-old to count a thousand bucks. But they eventually got there, setting up their second step.

"The first thing we must do with the money is give ten percent to the church," Kurt explained. After asking Kyle to read several Bible passages about giving, Kurt instructed them to count out one hundred dollars and place the bills in front of a picture of a church building.

"The Bible also says we are supposed to save—so I want you to count out another one hundred dollars to put in the bank." As the boys counted, I sensed Shaun starting to worry. After removing a second pile of bills, however, a fairly high percentage of the stash remained.

"Finally, the Bible teaches us to 'owe no man anything'—so we must pay our bills. Once we've done that, like I promised, you can spend this cash on anything in the world you'd like." The page listed several bills with dollar amounts required to pay for our house, our food, our car, our clothes, and other things. As the boys counted out the required amounts, color drained from Shaun's once eager face.

As you might imagine, the total brought the drain to nine hundred ninety-eight dollars, leaving a single bill for each boy's spending splurge. We ended our evening by helping the boys create allowance boxes with three sections—give, save, and spend—and teaching them the rhyme "Before you spend away—give, save, and pay!"

The next morning, Kurt rushed our life savings back to the bank.

Mini-Tip   MONEY MANAGEMENT

It is never too early to begin modeling and teaching your children about handling money. Why not start when they are young by setting up a give, save, and spend allowance box? You can also find helpful tools for teaching money management to young children by visiting www.crown.org and www.daveramsey.com.

CHAPTER 7

Mini-Hurts

REDEEMING PAINFUL TIMES

Shaun stands beside a classmate, dressed in western attire for the special country music performance. The awkward expression on his face shows his feelings about the straw hat he's wearing—not cool. Of course, we took advantage of the moment to snap a candid. Most people might consider the photo forgettable—more suited for the discard pile than the refrigerator door. But to me, it is a treasured keepsake.

Shaun has been image conscious practically from birth—always admiring the latest clothes, hairstyles, and hip lingo. Somehow, he knew the meaning of *cool* before he could say the word. At the age of three he used to scoot out to the edge of our front lawn on his tricycle in hopes of catching a glimpse at the older, cooler kindergartners walking past our house on the way to school. Those sporting edgy clothes or radical haircuts got a wave and a smooth "hi, there." Those who were too cute or perky didn't get the time of day. To excite Shaun when he was four, I took him shopping for a new shirt or pair of shoes. He insisted on going along to make sure he got the right look.

A bright, talented, sweet little guy, Shaun is definitely all boy. Only two years younger than Kyle, he always felt a bit competitive with his older brother. Some would call it sibling rivalry; we prefer "iron sharpening iron." Shaun lost enough wrestling matches with Kyle to develop a tough exterior. But underneath it, he has an extremely tender and vulnerable spirit.

One day, Kurt and I attended an all-school awards ceremony. You know, the kind where kids sit cross-legged on the gymnasium floor while camcorder-armed parents stand in the back, hoping to capture the big moment when their child's name gets called. Shaun sat with the other first graders, and his brother was a few rows up with the third grade class. Kurt and I stood in back, watching our sleeping baby with one eye and the ceremony with the other. Fifteen minutes into the program, we heard our Kyle's name called. I cheered while Kurt hit the record button. We were happy for Kyle, who had received several of these awards before, but worried for Shaun, wondering how he would feel if Kyle got an award but he didn't.

We held our breaths as the principal announced the first grade awards. When they reached the end of the list, Shaun remained seated.

Shaun pretended not to care, but his heart was crushed. (Why do they allow siblings to attend these ceremonies together anyway?) After the closing announcement we walked home, Kyle proudly displaying his certificate, Shaun tightly holding my hand.

"Maybe I'll get an award next time, right, Mom?"

Swallowing the lump in my throat, I willed a cheerful response.

"Right, sweetheart. Maybe next time."

Shaun forgot his disappointment within hours, thanks to heaps of sincere but overdone praise from his parents. But I will never forget it. Kyle's certificate went on display in his bedroom, gathering dust with the others. But the photograph of Shaun in his straw hat made our photo gallery—a reminder that no matter how tough he tries to appear on the outside, our second little boy has a very tender heart. And, while we may not be able to protect Shaun from award assemblies or other more traumatic tragedies, we can nurture his spirit—and buy him cool clothes.

One of the most difficult parts of mommyhood are times when we must helplessly watch our precious little ones endure painful experiences. Everything within me wants to shield my children from scraped knees, hurt feelings, high fevers, and crushing disappointments. But I can't. Sooner or later, painful times will come. My task is not to prevent them but to increase the odds my children will thrive in spite of them.

I find inspiration in this regard when recalling an incident that occurred in 1986. My husband's best boyhood friend, Don Beck, boarded a plane at Detroit's Metropolitan Airport—leaving his young bride and baby boy behind to extend their visit with family. But as the plane hurtled down the runway, it did not rise at the normal point; instead, it continued hundreds of feet farther before lifting almost fifty feet. The plane clipped the edge of a rental car building, ricocheted off the embankment of an access road to the interstate, and disintegrated into chunks of fiery metal.

More than one hundred passengers died that

day—including a young father leaving behind a grieving wife and a baby boy who would never know his daddy. But in the midst of tragic loss, a glimmer of hope emerged.

A child was found alive. According to one news account,* rescue workers found four-year-old Cecilia Cichan in a child's car seat, moaning amid the crash debris. Some assumed she had been in a car trapped beneath the plane. Instead, she turned out to be the sole surviving passenger.

While no one can know for certain, some rescuers believed that Cecilia's mother, Paula, saved her daughter's life by wrapping herself around the child's seat to protect her. Knowing she couldn't stop the tragedy, Paula presumably did her best to place her daughter in an environment that would increase her chances for survival.

I cannot prevent my children from going through pain and heartache in this life. But I can follow the example of Paula. Just as she wrapped her body around that precious little girl to absorb the impact and flames, I can wrap my children in the protective reassurance of my unconditional love.

When my children walk into our house, I want them to experience the kind of nurturing

---

*"Miracle Girl," *Time*, August 31, 1987.

environment I missed as a child. When Shaun comes home from a school awards assembly feeling like an academic failure, I want to be there for him emotionally—surrounding him with praise for his many talents. I might be having a bad day myself, feeling frustrated, unappreciated, or depressed. But he needs me to play a heroic part, shaking off my self-pity and leaving my seat to wrap myself around his fragile spirit. Only then can I increase his odds for survival; only then can I redeem painful times to help him thrive through the mini-hurts life inevitably will bring.

Mini-Tip

REFUGE

You never know when a mini-hurt will occur in your child's life. Quite often, those hurts are caused by an unkind classmate or some other person outside the protective walls of your home. Establish a set of family rules that make it clear to your children that your home is a refuge from the disrespect and survival-of-the-fittest mind-set common in the world. The rules can be whatever you think will affirm each child's identity and self-image—such as "No rude comments" or "No put-downs in jest," etc. The key is setting, modeling, and enforcing them.

CHAPTER 8

Mini-Sleeps

REVITALIZING BEDTIMES

Before entering the minivan years, going to bed was a relatively straightforward process: easy going, like driving on the open road with nothing to hinder a delightful trip. When I got tired, I slid between the sheets, closed my eyes, and escaped the cares of the world in a cloud of temporary indifference. Certainly, I had my share of late nights—especially during finals week in college or grading papers as an elementary school teacher. But once I crawled into bed, sleep took over.

Since having children, going to bed has been more like driving in heavy traffic—kind of a start–and-stop activity. When I get tired, I try to find the sheets buried somewhere beneath the pile of disheveled pillows and blankets. Before I can get there, I am summoned by the cry of a child. It might be a baby screaming for a bottle. It might be a toddler demanding a drink of water or a preschooler begging for "one more book" before they fall asleep. It might be all of the above in a single evening; start, stop, start, stop.

I must confess, on those nights when I am particularly exhausted from a long day catering to kid demands, I'm sometimes tempted to dole out doses of cough syrup thirty minutes before bedtime. Just once, I'd like to skip the bedtime routine of watering, reading, tucking, and retucking to hear nothing but the sweet sound of unconscious children in dreamland while I drift away beside my sleeping husband.

As it is, bedtime includes a long litany of obligations that must be met before I can close a single eye. And on the top of the list is a nightly routine that must be followed without amendment for four-year-old Nicole (and hence any of the rest of us) to get any sleep at all. It goes like this:

Step one: Floss and brush teeth.
Step two: Go potty. "I know you think you just went, but that was twelve hours ago. So try to go again so that you don't wet the bed!"

Step three: Eat a bowl of cereal. "What do you mean you're hungry? You just ate dinner two hours ago!"

Step four: Floss and brush, take two.

Step five: Read one book. "Okay, three books. But make them short ones!"

Step six: Crawl into bed and tuck in the sheets, Barbie blanket, and bedspread.

Step seven: Close the blinds and click on both small lamps with the green lightbulbs before turning off the main light. "Those are just shadows, not monsters on the wall."

Step eight: "You're right, sweetie, I did forget to pray. Let's hold hands . . ."

Step nine: Select a stuffed animal from dozens sitting atop the nightstand.

Step ten: Find the "go to sleep" music CD and start the first track. "No, I won't turn it up. This is loud enough."

Step eleven: Shut the door but not completely. There must be a three-inch crack to allow some of the hallway light in and Nicole's voice out in the case of some imagined emergency.

Step twelve: Wait just outside the door, since her first question, "What are we doing in the morning?" will come shortly.

Step thirteen: Repeat any preceding step as required.

Keep in mind, I am usually a walking zombie by the time I'm putting Nicole to bed. I just want her to fall asleep, fast. Then I want to go and do likewise. So, after several months following the same routine, I faced a crossroads: I could either commit myself to an asylum or recommit myself to making bedtime an enjoyable experience. I decided to choose option two and live on the wild side by making step nine more interesting.

I should explain that the process of selecting a stuffed animal for Nicole to sleep with takes much longer than it sounds. Because she likes the process more than the outcome, I found myself holding up one animal after another every evening until we went through the entire collection of twenty-something creatures. Only then would she choose.

Particularly tired one evening, I decided to out-smart my daughter by introducing a little game into our routine. They say necessity breeds invention. I selected two animals from the pile and gave each a voice. Taking turns, they begged a wide-eyed Nicole: "Please sleep with me!" "I'm better. Please pick me!"

Delighted by the animated conflict between potential bedtime companions, Nicole played right along. After momentary reflection, she chose Ms. Poofy Pink Bear—setting up my next big act.

"Will you sleep with me next time?" Winnie-the-Pooh's tearful voice inquired. "Pleeeeeeeease?"

As Nicole promised the next bedtime to Mr. Pooh, I grinned, because she had fallen right into my trap. Not only had I cut five minutes off our bedtime routine that night, I had eliminated step nine altogether for the following night!

Troy, then seven years old, had been watching the entire episode while waiting for me to finish up with Nicole so that we could begin his routine. As I glanced his way, Troy gave me a big smile of approval.

"Mom, you are the best! That was such a good idea. Nicole loved your mini-drama. I can't get over how fun and brilliant you can be when you put your mind to it. Two thumbs up!"

Okay, that might be a bit more than he said. But that's what I heard.

I had figured out yet another way to make life fun for my children. That I was tired and trying to cut down an extensive routine for my own interest is beside the point. All that Troy saw was Mom loving her kids enough to keep things interesting.

Now, if only I could figure out a way to make a spoonful of cough syrup seem like fun!

*   *   *

In the famous passage of Scripture in Deuteronomy commanding parents to introduce their children to God, we are told to talk about His commandments "when you lie down and when you get up" (6:7, NIV). He must have known about the endless process of lying down and getting back up that occurs every evening with young kids! I have resigned myself to the idea that parental exhaustion is part of His grand design, and my husband and I have tried to take advantage of bedtime to create and capture meaningful moments with our children.

For the little ones, we discovered something called bedtime blessings—a concept we learned from our good friend Dr. John Trent. John's book *The Blessing* highlights the importance of blessing our children in tangible ways, such as meaningful touch and words of affirmation. A great time to give both comes at the end of the day when I take my son or daughter onto my lap and read a favorite book together. What we read is not as important as the time we spend reading. As I've seen in the lives of all four kids, the time invested in unhurried, sweet interaction pays tremendous dividends in the child's emotional security.

After reading together, I pray with the child while gently touching his or her arm or shoulder. Often, that prayer is one I've taken from the book *Bedtime Blessings* Volume 2, a series of bedtime readings and prayers specifically designed to help moms and dads turn bedtime into a time of blessing. Here is a sample of one bedtime blessing you might try:*

Let's Play a Game
FUNNY BUNNY

Tonight's game is Funny Bunny. Funny Bunnies are word-pairs that rhyme. Like "funny bunny" or "kitten's mittens."

Here's how you play. One person thinks of a Funny Bunny, and then gives a clue to the other person so they can guess what it is. For example, I might be thinking of a "hoarse horse." My clue would be: "animal with a sore throat." Or, I tell you I'm thinking of an "animal's chuckle." The right answer would be a "calf's laugh."

Okay, I'll start.

[*Here are a few to get you going:*

tin bin
rat hat

---

*John T. Trent, *Bedtime Blessings*, vol. 2 (Colorado Springs: Focus on the Family Publishing, 2001), p. 86. Reprinted with permission.

boy's toys
dollar collar
mouse house
bear chair.]

Wasn't that fun? Let's see if we can think of Funny Bunny nicknames for each of us, before we spend time talking to God.

[*Use your first names, family names—Dad, Mom, Son, Daughter—or other words that describe you to create your rhyming nicknames.*]

Dear God,
Thank you for _____ [*your child's name*] and our family and the care You provide for each of us. Watch over us as we sleep and refresh us so tomorrow we can be alert to all the blessings You have in store for us.
Amen.

As you can see, the prayer allows parents to make the experience personal. In fact, Nicole often asked for "the book that is about me." I gladly obliged.

In another Bruner family bedtime tradition,

I lie next to one of the kids on their designated evening to chat for fifteen minutes before he or she drifts off to sleep. The topic of conversation is chosen by the child. We have found that some of the most profound spiritual discussions of the week occur during those fifteen minutes of uninterrupted dialogue.

As our older boys have evolved from lap-sitting kids to whisker-growing teens, bedtime has taken on a whole new personality. Once my husband and I finally get the little ones blessed and to sleep for the night, we enter our bedroom to find two lanky teens sitting on our bed to begin their nightly routine of connection. (For some reason, they most want to discuss the particulars of their day just when Kurt and I are ready to collapse or spend some private time together.) But neither of us mind; we recognize how important blessing our children through conversation can be. Those conversations have ranged from questions about God to school assignments to friend situations to current events.

And so it goes. Someday I will once again know what it means to get to bed at a decent hour. In the meantime, I'll continue trying to make bedtime in the Bruner family a blessed event.

Mini-Tip   ON THE SCHEDULE

Select which night per week you will lie down with each child and put it on the schedule. If it doesn't get on the calendar, it doesn't happen. If the child knows which evening is his or her designated slot, he or she will not expect it all the time. Also, when the child plans for a specific evening, he or she will remind you—holding you accountable to actually do what you might otherwise skip.

CHAPTER 9

Mini-Faith

INFLUENCING SPIRITUAL TIMES

At four years old, Nicole tried to understand and express one of the most profound mysteries of Christian faith—the doctrine of the Trinity. I know, I know—some of the greatest minds in the history of the church have argued and debated how best to articulate a single God in three persons. But Nicole found a way of cutting straight to the chase.

"Jesus lives in your heart."

Half talking to herself, she looked like she was trying to sort out a complicated algebra problem.

"God lives in your heart," Nicole continued. And then, as if suddenly fitting the puzzle pieces together, she smiled. "Jesus and God are in your heart. Both of those guys are!"

Well, she may have a bit of contemplation to go before fully grasping Christian theology. But she is hopefully well on her way.

As we were pulling out of the church parking lot one Sunday, Kurt asked then five-year-old Troy the first of two questions expected of every parent after Sunday school.

"How was class today?"

"Fine." A halfhearted reply.

My husband mindlessly spouted question two while looking into the rearview mirror.

"What was your lesson about?"

Troy glanced up from his incomplete craft paper project, mustering just enough apathy to reply.

"Oh, God again."

When Kurt first told me about the interchange, I chuckled at the naive innocence. Of course the lesson was about God! But then I became concerned. As a periodic substitute Sunday school teacher, I wondered how many kids sitting under my instruction yawned and responded similarly to their own parents. Am I—are we—boring kids with the most important truths in life?

Fast-forward several months to another scene. In the minivan on a four-hour drive, we listened with our children to the Focus on the Family Radio Theatre adaptation of *The Lion, the Witch, and the*

Wardrobe. As my husband described it, silence over-took all of us "as we endured the dreadful scene of Aslan's death on the stone table. A deep sadness rested upon nine-year-old Shaun as he absorbed the injustice and loss." Like so many children, he loved the great Lion—creator and defender of all that is good in Narnia.

Moments later, Shaun's grief turned to celebra-tion as he realized Aslan was alive again—risen from death to deal the evil White Witch a mortal blow. "The gloom of death overtaken by the delight of resurrec-tion, Shaun could not contain his excitement. 'That's just like Jesus!' he screamed from the backseat.

"Like most kids raised in Sunday School, Shaun had heard the story of Jesus' death and resurrection literally dozens of times. It had become routine, ex-pected, perhaps even boring." Following Troy's lead, he might have responded to Kurt's Sunday morn-ing question about his lesson with an apathetic "Oh, Jesus died and rose from the dead, again." "But through a fantasy tale that had none of what Lewis called 'stained-glass and Sunday School associations,' Shaun was caught off guard—surprised by the most wonderful and potent truth of Christian faith."*

*Kurt Bruner, "Birthing Narnia," *Boundless* Webzine, 2005, http://www.boundless.org/2005/articles/a0001182.cfm; C. S. Lewis, *On Stories and Other Essays on Literature*, edited by Walter Hooper (New York: Harcourt Brace Jovanovich, 1982).

Such is the power of story to baptize a child's imagination in truths better experienced than studied. It is one thing to sing Jesus choruses and memorize John 3:16, both of which are vitally important to every child's faith journey. It is another thing to hang on every word of an exciting tale that points to transcendent realities. While one can be useful, spoon-feeding truth to a child, the other makes him want to eat.

A recent survey by Public Agenda found that over 60 percent of parents want their kids to develop a strong religious faith.* Among Christians, passing the faith to children consistently ranks as a top parental concern. Kurt and I consider helping our children know and love God our highest priority. That's why we helped found the Heritage Builders Association (www.heritagebuilders.com) to provide moms and dads with the inspiration and tools necessary to turn that "want to" into reality. But first, we had to learn a thing or two ourselves about the heritage-passing process.

There is toothpaste all over the plastic-covered table. Our kids are having the time of their lives

---

*Steve Farkas, Jean Johnson, and Ann Duffett, with Leslie Wilson and Jackie Vine, *A Lot Easier Said Than Done: Parents Talk about Raising Children in Today's America* (N.p.: Public Agenda, 2002).

squeezing the paste out of the tubes—trying to expel every drop like Dad told them to. "Okay," says Kurt, slapping a twenty-dollar bill onto the table, "the first person to get the toothpaste back into their tube gets this money!"

Little hands begin working to shove the peppermint pile back into rolled-up tubes—with very limited success. We are in the midst of a weekly routine in the Bruner home during which Kurt and I spend time creating "impression points" with the kids.

"We can't do it, Dad!" protests then five-year-old Shaun.

"The Bible tells us that's just like your tongue. Once the words come out, it's impossible to get them back in. You need to be careful what you say, because you may wish you could take it back." An unforgettable impression has been made.

Impression points occur every day of our lives. Intentionally or not, we impress upon our children our values, preferences, beliefs, quirks, and concerns. It happens both through our talk and through our walk. When we do it right, we can turn them on to the things we believe. When we do it wrong, we can turn them off to the values we most hope they will embrace. So Kurt and I have tried to find ways of making this reality work for us, rather than against us, creating and capturing opportunities to impress upon Kyle, Shaun, Troy, and Nicole our values and beliefs.

Fast-forward to another impression point on a different evening.

The kids are all standing at the foot of the stairs, waiting eagerly for Dad's instructions from up top.

"I'll take you to Baskin-Robbins for ice cream if you can figure how to get up here." He has their attention. "But there are a few rules you must follow. First, you can't touch the stairs. Second, you can't touch the railing. Now, begin!"

After several contemplative moments, the youngest speaks up. "That's impossible, Dad! How can we get to where you are without touching the stairs or the railing?"

After some disgruntled agreement from the other kids, Troy gets an idea. "Hey, Dad. Come down here." Kurt walks down the stairs. "Now bend over while I get on your back. Okay, climb the stairs."

Bingo! Kurt proceeds to compare this simple game to how it is impossible for us to get to God on our own. But when we trust Christ's completed work on our behalf, we can get to heaven. Another lasting impression is made. After everyone takes a trip up the stairs on Dad's back, the whole gang piles into the minivan for a double scoop of mint chip.

Years ago, when our oldest was only five, Kurt and I learned to set aside time each week to intentionally impress our values and beliefs on the kids through a weekly ritual called "family night." By creating object-lesson-based games and activities that reinforce our faith, the kids have fun and we pass on our spiritual heritage. The power of family nights is twofold. First, it creates a formal time and setting within which we can instill spiritual truths and character qualities into our children's hearts. Rather than defer to the influence of peers and media, or abdicate faith training to the school and church, we create opportunities to teach our kids the things that matter most.

The second impact of family nights is perhaps even more significant than the first. Twenty to sixty minutes of formal fun and instruction can set up countless opportunities for informal reinforcement. These informal impression points do not have to be created, they just happen—at the dinner table, while riding in the car, while watching television, or any other parent/child time together. Once we have formally discussed a given family night topic, we naturally refer to those principles during the routine dialogues of everyday life.

I wasn't raised in a Christian family. But my husband grew up in the home of a Baptist deacon. Back then, parents were encouraged to invest in their children's spiritual development through a method called "family devotions." Motivated by guilt from the pastor's annual sermon on fathers taking spiritual leadership at home, Kurt's father did as he was "admonished." So little Kurt sat between his siblings for a ritual that always resulted in his becoming bored or getting scolded. Of course, it was all for his own good. But to a seven-year-old squirming ball of energy, the supposed benefits weren't obvious. Given the option, Kurt would have chosen a trip to the dentist over the routine of family devotions.

In their most honest moments, Kurt's parents had to agree. His dad would much rather watch the ball game. But guilt compelled him to force the kids to sit through his awkward presentation of a Bible lesson and prayer. Like most dads, he probably felt inadequate, ill-equipped, and embarrassed. It's unlikely this is what the Lord had in mind when He commanded us to "teach my commands to your children."

That's why we became excited about family nights as an alternative method of spiritual training in our home. And while we haven't always been consistent—averaging every second or third week despite scheduling one every week—over ten years our children have probably experienced a hundred different impression points that would not otherwise have occurred. Family night quickly became their favorite night of the week. In fact, we often heard them ask several times per week, "Can we have family night tonight?" Music to Dad's and Mom's ears!

Mini-Tip   START SOMEWHERE

Pull out your calendar and choose a day in the next two weeks when you will do something for your first family night. It can be as simple or complex as you want to make it, and there are many ideas available from sources like www.heritagebuilders.com. If your husband is hesitant or creativity challenged, go ahead and gather the necessary materials and plan the activities—allowing him to enter into the fun without pressure. They key is to get started, partnering with your husband on some kind of intentional effort to pass your beliefs to the kids.

CHAPTER 10

Mini-Choices

DECIPHERING UNCERTAIN TIMES

Let's be honest. We all use the space between our box spring and floor as storage. By my best estimate it had been at least two years since I had last looked under my bed. Like an archaeologist piecing together one unearthed shard after another, I approximated the date by dragging every last dust-laden item out from beneath our bed. It occurred during one of my organize-the-unseen obsessions—those rare days when I open neglected sock drawers, reorganize the board game closet, and wash the little grease catcher screen above the stove. I got like that around the time each baby came, somewhere between packing the "it could be any time now" overnight bag and my water breaking. It must be part of the nesting instinct. This instance had been triggered by discussions of a possible move. You can't sell a house with clutter under the beds because, well, for the same reason you want your kids wearing clean underwear in case they get in a car accident and are rushed to the hospital.

Anyway, I estimated it had been several years since I'd last cleaned under the bed, when I retrieved a blue, three-ring notebook filled with dozens of plastic protector sheets. Even before opening the cover I knew I had found a long-forgotten treasure; Shaun's Pokémon collection, circa 1999–2003.

At first I smiled. Then I grimaced, recalling the many conflicts surrounding that silly set of cards.

The Pokémon phenomenon hit the United States about the same time my second son hit third grade. As I understand, they had been wildly popular in Japan prior to being introduced here. Suddenly, with no advance warning to unsuspecting moms, we were confronted with something they didn't even hint at in *What to Expect When You're Expecting*. I joined thousands of other moms, frantically trying to figure out why our boys were suddenly obsessed with collecting cards that had demonic-looking cartoon characters on them with "special powers" to kill one another. On one hand, they might be a seductive tool luring our precious children into the waiting arms of evil itself! On the other hand, they might be innocent fun—sort of the new version of marbles. Like I said, *What to Expect* said nothing about it, so who knew?

I recall reading articles at the time, expressing concern about possible cultic influences behind the game. Fearing the worst, some of the moms at church forbade their kids to buy the cards. Lacking the time to investigate the whole phenomenon, I decided to join them. Better safe than sorry, I figured.

But then Shaun began applying the full-court press. He begged, using those sad *I'm the only kid on the planet who can't have Pokémon cards* eyes to wear me down. What mother can stand the thought of her son being the only kid on the planet without a toy? I broke down, promising Shaun that I would ask his father to buy a pack of cards to try them out himself. If Dad considered the cards harmless fun, all would be well. Kurt played a few rounds and despite a few disturbing images on several cards, he decided that it seemed like a cross between marbles and baseball trading cards. So we let Shaun buy a few packs with his own money and one stipulation: Mom and Dad would scan each deck to remove any characters we considered too gruesome or gross for young kids. Before we knew it, the blue notebook with plastic protector sheets became essential to keep track of the growing collection.

For a while Pokémon cards became a hot trading commodity. Some of the rarest cards could be resold at hobby and trading shops for a hundred dollars or more. Of course, one had to buy a thousand three-dollar-per-pack sets in order to find one of those hundred-dollar cards. Still, the possibility inspired millions of kids—my own included—to justify their investment.

The good news about what I now refer to as the Pokémon era was that it didn't last forever. The bad news is that, as we suspected, the craze died down before Shaun found a single valuable card. He eventually lost interest but not before amassing a worthless collection now on the scrap heap of childhood—causing me to wonder why I hadn't trusted my initial gut instinct instead of allowing such a silly, unproductive distraction.

Should I have an epidural or endure the pain of natural childbirth?

Should I nurse or bottle-feed?

Should I let the baby cry herself to sleep so she'll rest or intervene to avoid emotional trauma?

Should I use time-out or discipline by spanking?

Shall I potty train at two or wait until three?

Should I let him start kindergarten after his fifth birthday or wait until he is six?

These are just a few of the thousands of questions every mom faces in the early days of parenthood. They highlight the never-ending, sometimes perplexing options that confront us as we seek to balance a child's immediate demands or desires with what we think, or hope, will be in his best long-term interest.

Seeking advice provides some help. But more often than not, you get conflicting opinions from equally trusted sources. So what's a mother to do?

Adding complexity to the process, some questions come at us that have no precedent in the annals of mommyville council because they haven't existed before. The only thing a woman who served as one of my mentors said about Pokémon cards was "What are Pokémon cards?" Not much help.

The same thing happened with the Harry Potter phenomenon. Kyle fit squarely into the target age for that series when the first title hit nearly every boy's bookshelf in the English-speaking world. An avid reader, Kyle wanted to read Harry's magical adventures. Because the series was brand-new, I couldn't seek advice from those who had gone before. So we had to read the books ourselves to determine whether or not they would be appropriate for Kyle. Not exactly something we had time to do but necessary nonetheless.

And then came Troy, our sports nut. He wants to play (and is quite good at) every athletic game known to man. Do I let him enroll in YMCA basketball and hockey during the same season, or do I insist he pick one sport at a time? One adviser suggests strict limitations; another recommends maximizing his opportunities.

Nicole introduced a whole new set of questions. What about those Barbie dolls? Do they affirm a girl's interest in all things feminine, or do they make her think an impossibly proportioned body is the only acceptable shape? Again, it depends upon who you ask.

I suppose it is the curse of every mother to endure such uncertain times. No book will cover every possible topic. No mentor will have experienced every possible scenario. No Oprah, Dr. Phil, or Dr. Dobson show will have discussed every possible decision you must make. The tension between what a child wants and what he or she needs will always exist, putting us in the unenviable position of needing to use our best judgment, make a partially informed decision, or—when all else fails—hope for a lucky guess! One way or another, however, choices must be made.

So I have one bit of advice I wish I had absorbed when I first entered motherhood. It is not necessarily profound, and it won't likely change which direction I choose in any given situation. But I now consider it among the best advice I've ever received.

Relax! We must learn to worry less and trust our instincts more. After all, God has placed that child in your care because He trusts you to make good decisions. Not that you will be perfect in every choice. But you are the perfect mommy for your child. I know, because God chose you for his or her protection, nurture, and training.

And, confusing as they may be, He also chose you to make the occasional decision about allowing Pokémon, Harry Potter, and Barbie into your home. And if you make a different choice from other moms, so be it. As long as you do so with your child's best interests at heart, I think you'll come pretty close most of the time to the right decision.

And even if you don't, there is always room under the bed for another childhood collection that ended up being a waste of time and money but did your child no permanent damage!

Mini-Tip   GO WITH YOUR GUT

When faced with a decision that includes a variety of options for your child, do your best to gather wisdom from trusted mentors and friends. Take the time to do whatever research you can to learn the pros and the cons of each possibility and spend some time talking to God in prayer. Stir those ingredients into your decision stew and then go with your gut and trust your instincts when it comes to your child's best interests. It does no good to let various options and differing opinions paralyze you.

CHAPTER 11

Mini-Charms

CELEBRATING FEMININE TIMES

Nicole is all girl, through and through. Just walk into her bedroom and you'll see what I mean. It's decorated in pink, and contains dozens of stuffed animals. All of them, even Winnie-the-Pooh, have been given a girl's name. In her closet hangs dozens of frilly dresses that, when she is given the choice, trump any pair of shorts and shirt I could quickly pull from her drawer. And of course she must also wear matching shoes and hair clip.

Nicole owns a large collection of dolls with accessories and has several dress-up costumes that transform her into most of the Disney princess characters, a fairy with wings and wand, a cheerleader with pom-poms, or even Little Red Riding

Hood. Her toy box contains none of the boys' former playthings—no toy spiders or snakes, baseballs, or hockey equipment. Rather than a solid blue or black backpack like those her brothers carry, Nicole totes a Strawberry Shortcake bag. We couldn't even hand down one of the boys' bicycles. Hers is pink with streamers, not red with flames.

Kyle, Shaun, and Troy all participated in YMCA soccer, basketball, and other sports. Nicole, on the other hand, took gymnastics and dance lessons. She loves to pirouette around the house to whatever music happens to be playing at the time—often wearing tights and ballerina tutu.

Needless to say, Nicole brought a whole different culture to the Bruner parenting experience. After three boys, we thought we had the process down cold. We didn't. But we couldn't be more grateful. I recall the excitement we felt when the ultrasound technician told us we were having a girl.

"You mean you think we're having a girl," Kurt responded. After three boys, the odds were not in our favor. "I'll believe it," Kurt continued, "when I don't see *it*!"

We had been half protecting ourselves during the months leading up to Nicole's birth. "We'd love to have a girl," we told ourselves, "but would be just as excited with another little boy." But when

Nicole entered the world without "it," we realized just how much we had wanted a girl after all. I wept in gratitude to God for giving me a female ally in an otherwise masculine domain.

And I do mean masculine. When Troy was four years old his preschool teacher decided to teach the kids a dance to perform for the parents. Big mistake! As he watched the dainty moves Miss Deb expected him to mimic, Troy perceived a conspiracy to undermine his manhood. So he rebelled, throwing a tantrum of self defense that nearly got him expelled from snack time.

As much as Nicole is all girl, Troy is even more all boy. That's why a recent experience caught me by surprise. Seated beside each other on the couch one evening, Troy scooted close. He's never been much of a cuddler, so I enjoyed the gentle expression of affection from my otherwise rough and rugged eight-year-old.

"I love you, Mommy." He melted my heart.

"I love you, too, sweetheart," I replied.

He continued, in part childish ramblings, part love sonnet. "I love your hair, your smell, and the pretty clothes you wear." He smiled a satisfied smile, like a teenager relaxing after mustering the courage to express his affection for the cute girl.

Troy is the last boy you would expect to

appreciate feminine charm and beauty. But even he couldn't help expressing an admiration he himself couldn't understand at so young an age. All he knew is that Mommy is more appealing than Daddy. She has nicer hair, smells better, and wears prettier clothes. He doesn't know why, but he likes that in a woman.

Apparently, so does Shaun. I remember the time he announced that I was the "prettiest mom in the world." Touched by his childish admiration, I thanked him for such a sweet comment. Concerned that I thought his compliment mere flattery, he continued, "No, I mean it. I've seen a lot of them!"

Kyle also seems drawn to his mom's feminine charms, even if he finds himself confused by Dad's attraction to the same. He especially didn't understand the way Dad expressed it on Valentine's Day 2002 when Kurt decided to write me a series of six or seven love notes to be opened one hour apart, each celebrating a different womanly quality he appreciates in me—from my nurturing spirit to my soft skin to the maternal care I give our kids. As one might expect on a lover's holiday, the final card mentioned some unmentionables and came with a beautifully wrapped gift from Victoria's Secret attached.

Kyle watched in excited anticipation as I opened one card after another throughout the day. Everyone loves presents, even when they belong to some-one else. He could hardly wait for me to get to the final note and unwrap the gift. I finally opened the box and looked inside, so Kyle asked what I got.

After I explained, a look of perplexed disap-pointment on his face said it all.

"Dad!" he scolded, as if the whole thing had been a cruel gag. "You mean after spending so much time writing seven cards and making Mom wait all day for her gift, the only thing you gave her is a pair of underwear?"

Like I said, our boys appreciate feminine charms even if they don't yet understand why.

Kurt and I have always tried to model for and em-phasize to our kids the goodness and beauty of love between husband and wife. Part of that process is giv-ing them a healthy sense of sexual identity by affirm-ing the differences between the sexes. In order to do so, we capitalize on critical events in their lives.

Taking Nicole shopping to buy a frilly new dress or a cute outfit tells her it is good for a woman to feel feminine and pretty.

Bringing Troy to a professional sports event lets him admire the strength and aggression that are uniquely masculine, showing how his boy-ness re-flects the image of God.

Verbally praising the uniquely masculine or feminine qualities in Dad and Mom in front of the children reinforces their own gender qualities and celebrates the healthy attraction between the sexes. When Dad says about Mom, for example, "I think Mom is the prettiest girl in the world. I'm lucky she is my date!" or "Mom has such soft skin—I love to touch it!" Or when Mom says of Dad, "We are blessed to have a daddy who works so hard" or "You'll have to ask Daddy to lift that—he is stronger than Mommy."

We also try to model how to treat the opposite sex at home so that our children learn there are differences that should be respected. For example, make it clear that it is okay to tackle and punch Daddy for fun, but not Mommy. We let our boys know that Mommy and Sister deserve privacy when they are changing clothes and vice versa.

Kurt tries to model and enforce with the boys to watch their manners when with Mommy and Sister (no burping, gross jokes, etc.). When the time comes, I will teach Nicole to be discreet about feminine matters in front of the boys. In these small but important ways, we help our children learn that there is something about the opposite sex that is worthy of special treatment.

When Kurt was young, his mother did something

very wise while the family watched television together. Whenever there was a scene in which a man
and woman became intimate with each other his
mom would tell them to change the channel *if* the
couple was not married. If they were married, on the
other hand, they could watch the show. (Incidentally, this was in the days when they were restrained
about what was actually shown on television.) In this
small way, she made an important statement to help
her children understand that sex itself is not dirty or
wrong, only sex outside marriage.

The kids are content. The house is calm. Nothing
can disturb this serene setting. Until . . . Kurt sneaks
up behind me, wraps his arms around my waist,
and begins blowing in my ear, whispering sweet
nothings and kissing my neck. Before anyone has a
chance to stop us, we just might become embroiled
in a full blown "mush out." Mom and Dad are up to
it again! The kids react in playful horror.

"You guys are gross!"

"Yuck!"

"Not again!"

Translation: "It's wonderful knowing Mom and
Dad love each other."

You see, Kurt and I want our children to admire and appreciate that God made women and
men different from each other, and to respect the

mysterious beauty of intimacy between husband and wife. These things should make them smile, even when they don't entirely understand.

So I will continue trying to look and smell better than Dad.

I will do my best to teach our daughter feminine charms.

And if I'm lucky, I will enjoy a nice cuddle with my eight-year-old admirer every now and then.

Mini-Tip
CELEBRATE YOUR FEMININITY

Declare today Feminine Charms day and treat yourself to one or more of the following girlish activities:

- Take a nice, long bubble bath
- Replace your frumpy sweatshirt with a cute blouse— even if you know it won't stay clean very long
- Spend $15 at a local spa to have your toenails painted
- Rent a romantic comedy and make your husband watch it with you
- Go shopping for "a pair of underwear" at Victoria's Secret so your husband will be glad he watched the romantic comedy with you

CHAPTER 12

Mini-Sins

CORRECTING ERRANT TIMES

He said what?" I couldn't believe my ears.

"Paul told me Shaun said the *F* word." Not something any mom wants to hear from the school office.

"But he doesn't even know the *F* word." At least I didn't think he knew it. And even if he did, he'd probably heard it from Paul!

A bit of context. Paul was the fourth-grade bully and Shaun his primary prey. So when Paul got in trouble for kicking my son and filed a counter allegation about the aforementioned foul word, you can imagine my skepticism.

One other bit. The voice on the other end of the phone was Paul's mom—the school secretary.

"All I know is that Paul heard him say the *F* word." She believed her son. I couldn't believe mine would do such a thing. Since he was knee-high Shaun has been, by kid standards, a spiritual giant. His sensitivity to the things of God often caught me by surprise. And while we tried to teach him tact, his courageous faith resisted most attempts at restraint. Despite bold declarations of belief, however, Shaun is no angel. But I still couldn't imagine him using foul language at school. Which brings us back to the *F* word.

"I would never use the *F* word!" I could tell by the look in his eyes that he spoke the truth. Moms just know. But would the school administration believe him?

"Shaun, do you know what the *F* word is?" the Vice Principal inquired.

"Yes. It's the worst thing you can say in the whole world!"

"What is the *F* word?" she prodded further, suspecting childhood naïveté.

Sensing it was safe to utter the forbidden word since the adults asked him, Shaun answered, "I would never say *fudge flux* to anyone!"

No angel. But no demon either.

About a year later, in fact, Shaun announced his own tendency to "fall short of the glory of God."

It happened when Kurt became frustrated at some minor offense.

"Dad, I'm only nine!" Shaun gave his theologically insightful defense. "And kids sin every once in a while!"

An understatement if ever one was spoken. Every parent can attest to the reality that kids sin every once in a while.

If you've read my previous book *Playstation Nation*, you know that video games have been an issue in the Bruner home. It took me seven years to finally recognize the addictive nature of what I call "the digital drug." Even before my epiphany, however, I considered them a waste of time and brain cells. So we placed some pretty strict limitations on game time.

When our oldest was about seven, we spent a holiday vacation visiting Grandpa Otis and Grandma Gail's home where Kyle discovered their old Super Nintendo video game system. It had all the classics; Donkey Kong, Tetris, Duck Hunt, and, of course, Super Mario Brothers. The games called our son's name every second of the day, pleading with him to beat the next level, and the next, and the one after that. How on earth did any parent expect a child to live within a one-hour-per-day limit

with so many ducks to shoot, donkeys to kong, Tetris blocks to tet, and Marios to bounce?

Now, like every mom, I liked to give the kids
their allotted video game time during those peri-
ods of the day when the adults become busy with
boring grown-up activities like talking, cooking,
washing dishes, or napping. On about day three of
our visit, Gail and I began cleaning up the kitchen,
while Kurt rested in the bedroom. Otis relaxed in
the family room, while Kyle devoured his sixty
minutes in front of the screen. But one hour on
video games is like eating one Lay's potato chip. So
when his time ended, he wanted more.

"When my mommy gets done talking," Kyle informed Grandpa, "I'm going to ask her if I can play
another hour."

Aware of my game-time rule, Otis asked, "What
are you going to do if she says no?"

At that moment, a devious expression came over
Kyle's face. It was as if he had calculated his odds
based upon my state of distraction, the increased
likelihood of bending the rules during vacation,
and the support he hoped to receive from a sympa-
thetic grandpa.

"Well," he said in a hushed tone, "then I'll keep
asking and asking and asking some more until she
says yes!"

Otis still laughs whenever retelling that story. I chuckle myself. But I also use it to remind myself of an unpleasant reality, one best understood by relating an incident that occurred when Kyle was a toddler.

As every parent of a two-year-old can attest, little kids like to follow the exact same routine every night before going to sleep. In our home, that routine included Kyle grabbing a book from the shelf, toddling over to Daddy's lap, and demanding he read "dis one" before lights out. "Dis one" happened to be a little board book titled *All Mine, Bunny* that taught kids about sharing by illustrating the consequences of a demanding, selfish bunny's behavior.

After about the thirtieth night in a row of reading *All Mine, Bunny*, Kurt desperately tried to convince Kyle to let him read a different book. But "dis one" fit the nightly routine—or rather "nightly rut" as Kurt called it. *Oh, well,* he figured, *what better rut than to instill the value of sharing in one's toddler?*

On about day sixty-five of *All Mine, Bunny*, we invited some friends to the house for dinner. The couple had their own toddler, so we situated Kyle and their little boy in front of a pile of Fisher-Price toys in the next room while the four of us enjoyed a nice meal and much needed adult conversation.

During dessert, Kurt overheard Kyle say the word

"share" in the next room. Pleased that his father-son bonding time seemed to be paying off, Kurt smiled and continued the conversation. But then he heard it again. Unable to contain his excitement and pride, Kurt pushed back his chair and stood up.

"Excuse me," he interrupted, "but I need to see what is going on in the next room." Grinning with self-congratulation, his eyes met mine. "It seems our son has learned a thing or two about sharing, thanks to our nightly rut!"

Kurt walked toward the door and peered around the corner just in time to hear Kyle once again utter the word "share" in a very demanding tone as he forced a toy out of the younger child's hands.

"At that moment," Kurt soberly reflected, "I realized that my son had inherited a sinful nature—from Olivia!"

While I accept only half the blame, I can't argue. Our children did indeed receive hand-me-downs from their parents. And, unfortunately, those hand-me-downs include a little reality called sin. A reality, by the way, that has also surfaced in Kyle's younger siblings.

Like the time Shaun told us a barefaced lie, trying to cover something he had done wrong. Both caught up with him, and his effort to avoid the embarrassment of discovery became double trouble.

Hurt and angry, I saw in my son a tendency to deceive. A tendency, incidentally, I had at his age.

Or the time we found streaks of white spray paint across the front fender of our new minivan. We questioned all four kids and received four denials. But then six-year-old Troy's face shouted *I'm guilty!* (Moms just know.) His mischievous side had gotten the best of him, inspiring the worst in him.

Even Nicole, our sweet little princess, has her moments. For some strange reason she takes pleasure inflicting pain upon our dog. A kick, slap or overaggressive squeeze triggers a high-pitched yelp—which in turn triggers disciplinary action. She knows better. She understands the consequences. But she does it anyway. Go figure.

So we are four for four. That's right, 100 percent of our children have shown bad attitudes, said naughty words, hit unsuspecting playmates, and made wrong choices. Correction, we are six for six. After all, they had to inherit these tendencies from somewhere.

As author P. D. James noted in *Children of Men*, if you treat children like gods when they are young, they are likely to act like demons when grown. It is important that we understand why our little angels can so quickly become devils by developing a solid theology of children. In short, the Christian faith teaches us that we (and our kids) are spiritual beings created for the purpose of relationship with God. Because we are made in God's image, we have tremendous capacity for good. Due to the disease called sin, however, we tend toward evil. We've been given a free will, making each of us accountable to God for our choices.

So, when your child utters that first dirty word and you wonder Where did that come from? suspecting the neighbor kid—remember that your child is bent toward evil and may not be as innocent as you assumed.

When you catch them lying, cheating, being lazy, or kicking the dog—rather than ask why you are such a bad parent, remember that they descend from bad stock. "For all have sinned" the Bible affirms "and fall short of the glory of God."

The bad news is that we, and our children, are hardwired to sin. So expect it, correct it, and, when the child is old enough to grasp it—let him in on the good news.

> But God demonstrates His own love toward us, in that while we were still sinners, Christ died for us.
>
> ROMANS 5:8,
> NEW KING JAMES VERSION (NKJV)

Mini-Tip   AS EXPECTED

When you discover or catch your child doing something wrong, watch your reaction. We can easily become over-emotional, in part because we see it as a reflection on our parenting skills. Instead, learn to expect your children to sin. After all, they are sinners. It is important to be firm in discipline. But be careful to show grace in the moment of discovery, remaining calm to avoid an emotional scene. Take the time to instruct your child on why what he or she did was wrong and assign an appropriate consequence, keeping in mind that sinful behavior is the human condition.

Mini-Enemies

DISCUSSING DEVILISH TIMES

Kids have a knack for recognizing evil when they see something that suggests ominous, preying, dark forces in our world. Take, for example, a book I considered rather innocent, titled *Go Away, Big Green Monster*. It became a bedtime-ritual read in our family when Kyle was about three years old. Sure, the word "monster" is in the title and on every page. But the text reads "You can't scare me, Big, Green Monster." Like the Pixar/Disney animated feature *Monsters, Inc.*, this monster wouldn't dare generate nightmares. So you can imagine my surprise when Kyle made a correlation I hadn't.

"We know who the monster really is, don't we, Mom?"

Um, who he really is?

"The monster," Kyle continued, saving me from the embarrassment of having to confess ignorance, "is really Satan!"

It wouldn't be the last time the enemy of our mortal soul would come up in bedtime conversation. Some years later I became ensnared in yet another satanic dialogue. Even though it was well past bedtime, I kept my promise to lie on the bottom bunk next to then eight-year-old Kyle and talk before the boys fell asleep. Shaun, who was then six, lay on the top bunk. Despite being unable to see my face because the room was dark, he peered over the edge to ask me a very profound question.

"Mom, we are supposed to love everybody, right?"

"That's right, sweetie," I answered, unaware of a setup.

"What about Satan? Are we supposed to love Satan?"

Not quite sure of the proper theological response, I went with my gut instinct. "No! We aren't supposed to love Satan."

I was naively confident I'd satisfied a six-year-old, but Kyle chimed in to spoil my moment. "Yes we are, Mom! We're supposed to love everybody. We just aren't supposed to love what he does."

Wondering whether or not I'm qualified for this conversation, I fumbled for something to end it so we could all get to sleep.

"Well, are we or aren't we?" Shaun needed an answer or he would be up all night.

"We'll talk about it later. Now go to sleep," I said in a firm yet loving manner.

Lovely silence for about sixty seconds.

"If Satan was an angel who sinned, can other angels sin?" Kyle asked, raising the bar.

Where do they get these questions? Whatever happened to the days when "Now I lay me down to sleep" covered things?

Despite the challenge of answering such profound theological questions, I'm glad my children ask. After all, they need to understand that they have an enemy who, according to the Scriptures "walks about like a roaring lion, seeking whom he may devour" (I Peter 5:8, NKJV).

I think we too easily forget that we live in enemy-occupied territory. Our children are not growing up in a benign kingdom with few threats to their spiritual well-being. They are growing up in a fallen world that includes a devil—one who wants their souls in his possession. And his tried-and-true method for snaring them is something called rebellion.

Our four kids huddle close together eight feet below Dad. Kurt looks over the upstairs railing, waiting for the first sign of a foot, a hand, or any other body part to expose itself beyond the edge of a large umbrella. The plan: Wallop the first child who ventures from under the umbrella with my pile of Nerf balls and rolled-up socks. The reason: It's family night and the kids have come to expect such crazy activities. On this occasion, we hope to give them an experience that will help them understand submission to authority.

Earlier in the evening we read an odd Bible verse to the kids to set up our umbrella activity. "For rebellion is as the sin of witchcraft, and stubbornness is as iniquity and idolatry" (NKJV). The statement appears in 1 Samuel 15:23 amid a heated conversation between King Saul and Israel's spiritual leader, Samuel.

"Why would Samuel compare rebellion to witchcraft?" Kurt asks the family. "Do you see any similarity between the two?"

Blank stares tell me the connection is less than obvious.

"And I wonder why he described stubbornness as iniquity and idolatry?" Again perplexed expressions.

I'm not surprised. After all, few grown-ups see the link.

My oldest is first to venture out, convinced he can outrun his dad's fastball. Kurt is elated, nailing Kyle's scrawny frame three times. The younger kids laugh at their brother's arrogance and huddle more tightly together. As we explain later, the umbrella represents authority—something God places over us to protect us from the dangerous forces of Satan's schemes. We read the scriptural admonitions to be on guard against the "fiery darts" of a devil who seeks "whom he may devour" (Ephesians 6:16, NIV). We learn of the need to submit to God and resist the devil. And we will discover why God gave the gift of authority—which brings us back to the story of Saul and Samuel.

God had instructed Saul to "utterly destroy" the Amalekites: every soldier, every citizen, every animal and, of course, their wicked king. During the battle, however, Saul made a slight change in the plan. Rather than kill everyone and everything, he brought back a few victory spoils. When Samuel confronted Saul, Saul proudly explained his "better idea" to Samuel.

"Be quiet!" came Samuel's angry response. "The Lord sent you on a mission. . . . Why then did you not obey? . . . Why did you do evil in the sight of the Lord?" (1 Samuel 15:16–19, NKJV)

Not obey? Do evil? Samuel's reaction seems a bit harsh. After all, everyone else brings back spoils after defeating an enemy. And being such a thoughtful guy, Saul only wanted to offer a nice sacrifice to the Lord.

Samuel doesn't buy it. "Behold, to obey is better than sacrifice. . . . For rebellion is as the sin of witchcraft, and stubbornness is as iniquity and idolatry" (1 Samuel 15:22–23, NKJV).

Like my oldest son venturing beyond the umbrella, Saul had removed himself from the protective cover of God's clear command. As a result, he got walloped with a harsh consequence.

Why does Samuel compare rebellion to witchcraft and idolatry? What do conjuring up spells and worshipping idols have to do with disobedience?

Witchcraft involves willingly placing oneself under the authority and influence of forces other than God in order to manipulate rather than submit to the supernatural. Idolatry, in similar manner, involves worshipping something other than God in pursuit of "benefits" beyond those He allows.

Rebellion is also removing oneself from God's

protective authority. Once we step out from under the umbrella, we are fair game for the enemy. The pattern is as old as humanity.

Adam chose knowledge beyond innocence. Along with it came the "darts" of sickness, sorrow, conflict, and death. Thousands of years later that fateful choice influences my own home, including my four precious kids. Kurt and I want them to know that God established authority for our protection and guidance toward the kind of life we were made to enjoy.

He provides spiritual authority to shepherd their hearts: "Obey those who rule over you, and be submissive, for they watch out for your souls" (Hebrews 13:17, NKJV).

Civil authority to maintain social order: "Therefore, submit yourselves to every ordinance of man for the Lord's sake, whether to the king as supreme, or to governors, as to those who are sent by him for the punishment of evildoers and for the praise of those who do good" (1 Peter 2:13–14, NKJV).

And parental authority is the first of many umbrellas shielding them from harm.

"Children, obey your parents in the Lord, for this is right" (Ephesians 6:1, NKJV).

We want our children to understand that everyone will ultimately serve someone. We can either enjoy the freedom of serving the God who loves us or descend into slavery by serving an enemy who would love to blast us. But the Lord won't force any of us to stay under the protective guidance of authority, any more than he will intervene when the enemy's Nerf balls fly.

Mini-Tip READ UP

Brush up on the reality of our enemy by reading several biblical passages that describe his nature and schemes. After all, it is difficult to teach our children about something we ourselves don't understand. If your children are old enough, go through these passages together so that the entire family learns to be on guard while living in enemy-occupied territory.

- Ephesians 6:11–12
- I Peter 5:8
- Matthew 4:1–11
- John 8:44
- 2 Corinthians 11:14

CHAPTER 14

Mini-Jurisdictions

A few days before her first day of kindergarten, Nicole got a reflective look on her face while I hurriedly got her dressed before getting us both into the car for our latest errand run. It had been yet another busy season in the Bruner family when several to do list items remained, well, *to do*. I probably seemed more intense than usual, certainly more intent. A brief rundown of the week's conversation:

"Nicole, I told you to get your shoes on. We're going to be late!"

"I'm sorry, sweetheart, I can't play right now—I have to get dinner ready."

"Yes, we have to wash your hair again. You don't want to get bugs on your head, do you?"

"Nicole, you need to put your toys away before we leave."

"Okay, but just one book. It's late and we have to get to bed."

You get the picture. Poor Nicole. The crazy schedules of her three older brothers had forced most of the fun out of my playful personality, turning me into more of a demanding boss than a nurturing mommy. Which brings me back to the reflective look on her face.

"Mommy," she began, glancing up at me while fastening the Velcro straps on her shoes. "How did you grow into a mommy so fast?"

A strange question since, in her eyes, I had never not been a mommy.

"Well, I used to be a little girl like you. Then I grew up, got married, and became a mommy. Why do you ask?"

"I want to be a mommy," came her precious reply. The process of growing up was taking too long—and she couldn't wait to become a mommy. I apparently retained some stature in her eyes beyond that of household tyrant.

"Oh, that's nice, Nicole. Why do you want to be a mommy?"

"So I can be in charge of everything," Nicole said boldly.

Being the baby of the family meant bearing the brunt of everybody's demands—including my own. She didn't aspire to mommy's loving persona. She wanted mommy's absolute power!

"Everything," she quickly corrected herself, "except for Daddy."

Almost absolute power. But being in charge of everything "except for Daddy" is still pretty powerful from a five-year-old's perspective.

Of course, the daddy exception is a mere technicality. She doesn't realize just how much influence I have over even his actions and decisions. Every self-respecting woman knows the power of the right look, word, or touch. But we'll leave that aside for the moment. Suffice it to say that Mommy's authority goes pretty far.

Several years ago our older boys learned about family jurisdictional boundaries when Dad sacrificed influence in one major department, thanks to willful negligence. About ages seven and five, Kyle and Shaun had their first "guy's weekend" with Dad while I went out of town to visit my best friend back home in Oregon. I can't tell you how nice it was driving away from the house knowing I would enjoy three and a half days relaxing in my old stomping grounds, knowing I didn't have to worry about the kids because they were with my husband. I could read, chat, and rest secure in the knowledge Kurt had everything under control.

The trip turned out to be all that I'd expected and needed, allowing me to come home refreshed and ready for another tour of duty in mommyville. And as an added bonus, I discovered just how essential I am to my children's survival.

In order to celebrate my return and thank Kurt for giving me a break, I decided to cook one of the family's favorite meals—roast beef, mashed potatoes, corn, and French bread. We sat down at the table, gave thanks, and the boys dived in. And I do mean dived! I had never seen them eat so voraciously. They ate a lot and moaned in delight after each bite, as if they had never tasted such heavenly food in their lives. If I didn't know better, I would have thought Kurt had starved them all weekend.

I didn't know better.

"They sure seem hungry tonight," I teased Kurt between bites. "You did feed them while I was gone, didn't you?"

"Of course," he answered defensively. "They ate three meals a day."

"What did they eat?" I inquired, having earlier

noticed the food I had left for Kurt to cook was un-disturbed in the refrigerator.

"Well, let me think for a moment." He leaned back in his chair to reflect upon the past few days. I saw him counting silently on his fingers, as if re-hearsing each meal in his mind to make sure all nine were accounted for. With each finger, the look on his face became more sheepish.

"So?" I pushed for the verdict.

"Well, every time I got ready to fix something, I asked the boys what they wanted to eat." Mistake number one.

"And they never wanted what you had planned." Excuse number one.

"So I gave them what they wanted." Mistake number two.

"And what did they want?" I pushed on the door he hoped to keep locked.

"Funny thing is, now that I think about it, they always wanted the same thing."

"Which was?"

He didn't need to respond. The boys volunteered the information I might have guessed. "Cereal!" they shouted in unison.

That's right. Over the nearly four days I had been gone, my children had eaten nothing but dry cereal with milk. No wonder they consumed the food on their plates like wild animals devouring prey. A child needs protein, for heaven's sake! Something they hadn't had since saying good-bye to Mommy.

At that moment, Dad forfeited jurisdictional authority in the family kitchen. He is still allowed the occasional breakfast decision, an area in which he has proven himself all too capable. But when it comes to the important decisions about the kids' nourishment, I am the clear and undisputed leader. Years later, the family still jokes that no matter what other areas Dad may control, Mom will always be the boss of food.

If you want to lob a grenade into an otherwise pleasant conversation, bring up the topic of wives submitting to their husband's authority in the home. My generation of women, even those raised in Christian churches, automatically bristle at the notion. We, like Nicole, want to think of Mom as the one with all the power. If she does allow her husband the illusion of authority, it is only because it helps preserve his fragile male ego.

Perhaps you've heard the story, but it bears repeating. An angel holding a golden clipboard stood before an assembly of heavenly residents on the opening day of eternity. Hoping to organize the crowd into groups based upon their earthly performance, the angel gave what he thought was a clear set of instructions.

"I need all the married men to form two lines," he began. "Those who were henpecked, weak leaders who allowed their wives to rule the roost, step to the right. Those who authoritatively ruled their homes like a man's man, form a line to my left."

A long, winding line formed to the right as one honest husband after another admitted his weakness. Before long, every man in the crowd stood on the angel's right. Every man, that is, with the exception of one solitary man standing at the left.

"What is your name, son?" the angel asked.

"My name is Fred, sir," came the man's reply.

The angel looked to the right at a line of what must have been millions of men honest enough to admit they had not truly led their homes, allowing their wives to "wear the pants in the family." The angel turned back to Fred, standing alone, and he wondered whether Fred had heard properly.

"Let me make sure you understood my instructions," the angel said. "This line is for all men who wore the pants in their families, who ruled with iron fists, and who kept their wives in their places."

"Yes, sir," came Fred's reply.

"Well, I can't help wondering why you are the only one out of millions of men who chooses to stand in this line. Do you really expect me to believe you are the lone man's man in this entire assembly?"

"Believe what you will, sir," Fred answered. "All I know is that after you gave the instructions, my wife told me I had to stand here."

We laugh, in part because the scenario is not that far off from reality.

I won't go into all the theological arguments for and against male leadership at home. Those who accept biblical authority know what I'm talking about. Suffice it to say, God established jurisdictional authority in every institution—government, the church, and the home. He gave the husband authority and responsibility. And while some abdicate that role, most do their best to fulfill the job description detailed in Paul's letter to the Ephesians:

> Husbands, love your wives, just as Christ loved the church and gave himself up for her.
>
> EPHESIANS 5:25, NIV

> Fathers, do not exasperate your children;
> instead, bring them up in the training
> and instruction of the Lord.
>
> EPHESIANS 6:4, NIV

I grew up in a family where the man didn't fulfill these roles. My father was abusive to my mother, hardly loving his wife as Christ loved the church. And definitely exasperating his children. So I am by no means ignorant of how badly some men mess up their end of the bargain.

Because I am a wife, however, my concern is over us wives messing up our end.

> Wives, submit to your husbands as to the
> Lord. For the husband is the head of the
> wife as Christ is the head of the church,
> his body, of which he is the Savior. Now
> as the church submits to Christ, so also
> wives should submit to their husbands
> in everything.
>
> EPHESIANS 5:22–24, NIV

In everything? Does the Lord have any idea what that would mean in my family? The kids would waste away from eating nothing but cereal!

In all seriousness, this submission thing is much easier said than done. I especially find it a difficult concept, since I had no model during my child-hood of the kind of mutual submission God in-tended fathers and mothers to demonstrate. But I want something better for my children than what I received.

I believe my jurisdiction in the home has little to do with lines of authority or my work outside the home. (Kurt and I have almost never had a seri-ous disagreement about a big decision, which is the only time the trump card of authority becomes an issue.)

The question to ask is not Who is boss of whom? but rather Who is responsible for what?

Kurt is responsible for modeling manhood, fa-therhood, and what it means to heroically sacri-fice himself for his family the way Christ sacrificed Himself for our redemption. Self-sacrifice comes in all shapes and sizes, such as Kurt providing for the family or when he plays with the kids after an ex-hausting day at work instead of crashing in front of the television.

I am responsible for modeling femininity, ma-ternity, and what it means to heroically sacrifice myself by serving my husband and my children. I serve Kurt when I show him respect and allow him to lead. I serve the kids when I play my role as the life giver of our home. I owe it to them to shake myself out of selfishness and choose a joyful attitude—allowing them to experience a home filled with love and affirmation rather than tension and angst.

So I can affirm Nicole's aspirations toward motherhood. After all, we moms may not be the final authority on all matters in the home. But our jurisdiction reaches pretty doggone far.

Mini-Tip PLAY TO YOUR STRENGTHS

During your next date night, sit down with your husband and discuss what strengths each of you possess in order to proactively decide who should take jurisdiction over what areas. If your husband, unlike mine, is a terrific chef—let him take the kitchen reins. If you are an accounting whiz, by all means manage the family finances. According to the Bible, we wives were created to be our husbands' helpmates by combining our areas of strength with his to produce a well-run household.

CHAPTER 15

Mini-Scholars

CHOOSING-A-SCHOOL TIMES

The background image on our home office computer monitor is a picture of Nicole sitting at her kindergarten desk. Her feet are crossed beneath the chair and her brand-new box of crayons sits before her. Wearing a blue beret to match the school uniform, a white blouse, and solid blue skirt, she looks too cute and older than I wanted her to be. I suppose no mom properly prepares herself for their last child's first day of school. It was hard enough facing the first child's first day of school. That occurred eleven years earlier when Kyle entered Antelope Trails Elementary—one block from our house but one hundred miles from my care and protection.

For some reason, taking Shaun and Troy to kindergarten seemed less painful than taking Kyle. I suppose experience helps. You quickly figure out that children come back home at the end of the day, usually in one piece.

But Nicole's first day of school caught me off guard. She was excited about her new clothes, new backpack, new supplies, and new routine, and she and I had been looking forward to the day for months. All summer long we counted the "dark naps" remaining until the start of school. ("Dark nap" is what Nicole calls the eight-hour sleep we do at night, in contrast to the brief "light naps" she takes after lunch.) So I expected an easy, in-and-out process. After all, I had the routine down pat after three prior launches:

Meet the teacher
Organize school supplies into the cramped desk
    space
Figure out where to hang the coat
Peer into the restroom to discover a nifty, five-year-
    old-sized toilet

Same steps. Similar room. But this time seemed less routine, more ominous. As I kissed Nicole good-bye, I felt a twinge of grief. Not worry like with the boys. Grief—like a precious season of life was coming to a close.

My husband felt worse than I did. For some time Kurt had been complaining to Nicole about her growing up. "Look at how big you're getting, Nicole," he teased. "I thought I told you I wanted you to stay small so that you could always be my little princess!"

"Daddy!" came Nicole's indignant reply. "I can still be your princess when I'm big. You know I have to grow up so I can go to kindergarten!"

Precisely the thing he dreaded. The arrival of "K day" meant Kurt had to reluctantly accept the inevitable. No matter how much he resisted, Nicole would indeed grow up. Of course, in her daddy's mind, sending her to kindergarten was just the first in a depressing series of events—including high school, college, marriage, and Kurt lying cold and lonely in an unmarked grave.

To add insult to injury, Nicole expressed a desire to accelerate her pace of maturation. It came wrapped in a less-than-positive assessment of day one.

"Mom," she began, hands on her hips, "I thought kindergarten was going to be fun!"

"You didn't like your first day?" I asked.

"You said we would do work," she continued, "but coloring isn't work!"

So much for the excitement of crafts. Nicole wants to jump right to algebra!

We took a lot of pictures on that last first day of school. With the boys we took the candid of each standing next to his first teacher. Nicole, on the other hand, has an entire collection.

Nicole beside Mrs. Myers standing by the classroom door

Nicole standing by the classroom door alone

Nicole standing by the classroom door alone in a wide-angle shot

Nicole sitting at her desk with crayons

Yet another of her at her desk emptying the supply box

Nicole standing in front of the trunk of a giant, papier-mâché tree whose branches sprawl across the entire ceiling

And in every photo, Nicole looks very grown-up.

No matter how we feel about the process, managing our children's education is a big part of what it means to be parents. And, more often than not, the mom does the majority of the managing—enrolling, proofreading, signing, carpooling, lunch packing, snack sending, and of course, bake sale volunteering.

The job of managing educational times has become dramatically more complex in recent years thanks to the school choice movement. Don't get me wrong: I am very happy about this development, even if it means more work.

For those unfamiliar with the concept, I'll use a simple contrast. When most of us were kids, parents had two options when it came to educating their kids: send them to the local public school or let them wallow in ignorance their entire life. Thankfully, my mom chose option one. So I attended the school based upon my street address, not based upon what best fit my needs. Kind of a one-size-fits-all strategy—like Henry Ford said, people could get his Model T in any color they wanted, as long as it was black. Efficiency was the name of the game, not choice.

Today, parents face a very different reality. The good news? We have lots of choices when it comes to how we educate our kids. The bad news? We have lots of options when it comes to how we educate our kids. Here are just a few:

- Send them to the neighborhood public school
- Put them on a waiting list for one of the district choice schools
- Enroll them in a charter public school
- Pay for them to go to a private religious school

- Pay for them to attend a private, nonreligious school
- Homeschool them using customized curriculum
- Homeschool them using prepackaged curriculum
- Teach them at home in partnership with a public charter school program
- Mix and match any combination of the above

Kurt and I have used most of these options with our kids, with the exception of paying for private education. But I did teach in a private school for several years, so have been exposed to them all on one level or other. Based upon our experience, I can say this about educating children: The best program is the one the parent actively chooses. And the best system is the one that gives parents as many choices as is feasible.

Why? Because, if nothing else, it makes an important statement to parents: You have your child's best interest in mind, so you choose. And it makes an important statement to politicians, school boards, curriculum developers, and teachers: You are here to serve parents as they educate their children, not the other way around.

When it comes to educating our kids, one thing is certain: They learn far more from us than they do from others. Just think about the vitally important life lessons that occur in the few years before school options even hit your radar screen.

Lesson one: Life is hard! This vital lesson occurs moments after exiting the nurturing safety of mommy's womb. Having grown accustomed to mommy's voice penetrating the thin wall of her tummy, baby has no reason to expect anything but continued comfort and warmth. Instead, baby feels huge fingers pulling her head out a too-small opening just before being hit by a blast of chilly air from what turns out to be a sterile delivery room filled with masked giants. Next, one of the giants decides to stick a sucking apparatus into her nose and mouth to extract fluid and then hangs her upside down and administers an undeserved spanking. When baby finally escapes the rough clutches of the impersonal giants and enters the comforting arms of her mom, what does she find? Her mommy is bawling like a baby! Confirmation that this postwomb existence must be hard for everyone.

Lesson two: Whining works! Lesson two starts right away as baby discovers that a good, loud cry solves all kinds of problems. Wet diapers become dry. Empty bellies become full. Boredom is relieved by giants making silly faces and talking in high-pitched voices. The child will find whining a useful tool for getting what he wants even' after infancy. Stuck in an uncomfortable car seat too long? A prolonged, irritating whine might just get you a kiddie ice cream cone. Jealous because big brother got a birthday present and you didn't? A pitiful, "nobody loves me" whine might just trigger a visit to a store to pick out a little something for yourself. For these and a thousand other reasons, a child must learn the art of effective whining as early as possible.

Lesson three: Sounds make words! One of the most amazing lessons of all is the art of language. It turns out that what seemed mere random noises coming from the mouths of giants can be used for intentional, structured communication—very handy when you want more than a fresh diaper or ice cream. To say a word or two and have someone understand your deepest longings or self-centered cravings is a wonder indeed. Even more exciting—best experienced sitting on mommy's lap—is discovering a bunch of those sounds written in something called a book.

The beauty of these and other lessons that occur before a child begins formal education is that they require a mommy's constant presence. From crying together in the hospital to reading together at bedtime, the child's first and best teacher is always by his or her side—cheering and guiding a process that will culminate in a walk across some high school or college platform in cap and gown before entering the grown-up world of a job, a marriage, and, hopefully, another mini-scholar or two eager to learn.

But that will be another day. For now, I must gather Nicole's jacket and backpack, load her into the car, and take her to school. Because, after all, I am responsible for making sure my children learn.

Mini-Tip   TAKE CONTROL

You are the best person to make educational choices for your child. View the school system, professional educators, and other resources as helpful partners—but do not abdicate your role to anyone else. There is no cookie-cutter plan that will work for every child or family, so feel free to ask questions and discover options—but don't feel guilty if your choice is different from that of other parents.

Mini-Heroics

LIVING SACRIFICIAL TIMES

Have you ever thanked your mom for potty training you? Me neither. After rescuing all of my own kids from the humiliation of a lifetime in diapers, however, I now realize just how much sacrifice it requires—and how much I owe my mom.

The potty-training years are among the most exhausting in life. Mine started in the summer of 1993 just before Kyle approached his third birthday. I had been eager to get him out of diapers since the day our second child was born, doubling the diaper budget and diaper-changing demands. I also wanted to beat the three-year-old deadline, since it seemed outside the respectable age limit for any child not to have moved beyond messy pants.

My mother-in-law told me that her kids began using the toilet before age two. You can imagine how embarrassing it was to have a son falling so far behind his father's accomplishment. So I purchased a stack of pull-up diapers, placed the potty in the bathroom, and started down the road determined to never look back.

A friend loaned me her copy of *Toilet Training in Less Than a Day*. What mom could resist the promise of such a title? Similar books have been released since then, including the slightly less ambitious *Potty Train in Three Days* and the slightly more appealing *Potty Train Your Child in Just One Day: Proven Secrets of the Potty Pro*. Who wouldn't want to achieve the status of potty pro?

I got excited. Like millions of other moms, I was determined to move my child beyond the smells and headaches of diapers in one day. Yeah, right! I still feel set up, deceived, betrayed, and hoodwinked. You see, they don't tell you what to do when the child fails to share his mom's enthusiasm. Kyle made it clear that he preferred a more cautious, gradual approach. Why rush such a big change? After all, diapers are our friends.

The war was on.

PHASE ONE: PROPAGANDA

Like any great army facing an entrenched enemy, I decided to launch a sustained propaganda initiative. By making the toilet sound like fun, perhaps Kyle would lay down his weapons and willingly surrender his position. Unfortunately, my son quickly saw through my ploy and dug his heels in further. Perhaps I would have had more success had I had access to some of those newly developed weapons, like Potty Elmo, the Potty Scotty Kit, or *The Potty Song* CD. But none of those had been invented yet, so I had to rely on floating Cheerios.

PHASE TWO: INVASION

Hoping I had worn down the enemy's defenses, I moved into the next phase of my battle plan. Like the Potty Pro book had suggested, I set aside an entire day to remain by Kyle's side. For the first time, he slid into a pair of big boy pants instead of a diaper, and I invited him to let me know when he felt the need to wee wee or poo poo and we'd have fun together sinking cereal ships floating in the toilet bowl sea. Remain by his side at all times! That was the key. So, other than the times I had to feed or change the baby, that's exactly what I did.

PHASE THREE: REINFORCEMENTS

Of course, while I was feeding or changing the baby, Kyle took advantage of the moment and messed his pants. As any parent who has used training pants will tell you, it is much easier to clean messes neatly contained within a disposable diaper than it is to clean up messes only moderately captured inside big boy pants. So, like any courageous soldier would do, I called in reinforcements. The moment my husband returned home from the office, we teamed up to keep Kyle from taking advantage of distraction for a surprise attack.

PHASE FOUR: RETREAT

I had no idea children could hold it for so long. Kyle absolutely refused to go to the bathroom during the day. He waited until nighttime when we were sleeping and messed both his big boy pants and his sheets. We began to think maybe diapers were our friends after all. So, on day six of our one-day potty-training program, we gave up and sounded the retreat.

Several weeks after Kyle's victory, I discovered a point of vulnerability. We had given Kyle a Reader Rabbit educational software program. Kyle fell in love with the program and played it every afternoon. I noticed that he came to me for a diaper change whenever he had finished the game. It occurred to me that Reader Rabbit time had evolved into his go-number-two routine. The next day, I placed the training toilet atop the office chair, removed Kyle's diaper, and sat him down to play the game. It turned out to be a stroke of genius. Within minutes the plop, plop of poo poo falling into the potty opened an exciting new phase of Kyle's life, reinstating his big boy pants and preserving my sanity.

I won't go into the details on my other three. Suffice it to say, each child was more stubborn and more resourceful than the previous. By the time we got Nicole out of diapers, I had the Potty Pro equivalent of a master's degree in child manipulation.

Surprisingly, I also had a much better understanding of the Gospel.

Shortly after reaching the pinnacle of popularity—thanks to calming a storm, casting out demons, raising the dead, and feeding thousands—Jesus caused his fan club to dwindle by telling them more than they wanted to hear.

"If anyone would come after me," he began, "let him deny himself and take up his cross daily and follow me" (Luke 9:23, English Standard Version [ESV]).

I can just hear the crowd's reaction. *A cross? What on earth is this guy talking about? Crosses are those horrid death instruments the Romans use to torture and kill criminals. Why would the rabbi want us to have anything to do with a cross?*

As if talk of crosses weren't bad enough, Jesus went on to make things even more confusing when he said, "For whoever would save his life will lose it, but whoever loses his life for my sake will save it" (Luke 9:24, ESV).

Save to lose? Lose to save? Has this guy lost his mind? Rolling their eyes and turning their heads toward home, many in the audience must have considered the statement nonsensical. Counter to every fiber of their being and every lesson of common sense, Jesus suggested they should set aside their own interests, security, and gain in exchange for the opportunity to bear a cross.

Nice offer, Jesus. But we'll pass on that one, thank you.

The theme continued to emerge, such as when He said that a seed must go into the ground and die in order to bear fruit, adding that "Whoever loves his life loses it, and whoever hates his life in this world will keep it for eternal life" (John 12:24–25, ESV).

He made it clearer after alerting the disciples to His own pending death, reminding them, "Whoever seeks to preserve his life will lose it, but whoever loses his life will keep it" (Luke 17:33, ESV).

What does it mean? How do we keep by losing?

Was Jesus referring to *His* death or *my* life? Should I ponder His words as a mysterious paradox or live them as practical reality?

I believe the answer comes when we understand that Jesus was doing more than teaching us abstract concepts. He was inviting us to play a part in His great work of redemption by replacing the tyrant of petty self-absorption with a life of heroic self-sacrifice. The cross is more than a symbol of my salvation. It is also the symbol of every parent's calling.

I recall the story of a boy named Bobby and his younger brother who peered over the kitchen counter, watching their mother prepare breakfast. As she slipped the first golden pancake onto a plate, the older brother quickly tried to stake his claim. "I get the first pancake!"

Disappointed by her son's self-centeredness, Mom used the occasion to teach an important life lesson. Looking into the eyes of her oldest son she said, "Now, Bobby, if Jesus were here right now He would say, 'That's okay. Let my brother have the first pancake. I will wait for the next one.'"

After a moment of reflection, Bobby looked down at his younger brother, Billy, and excitedly proclaimed, "Billy, you be Jesus!"

I suppose we all want to be like Jesus until we

realize it means questioning some of our fundamental assumptions about how we really achieve a meaningful life.

Are women doomed to discontent if they wed Joe Ordinary rather than Prince Charming or nurture children instead of pamper themselves? If so, why did Mary—the most celebrated woman in history—call herself a servant "of humble estate" who sacrificed everything she wanted in order to give life to a precious child and a dying world?

We find our lives when we learn that the path to real meaning goes far beyond fulfilling one's personal passion. It is found in the kind of self-sacrifice modeled in Christ's Passion—laying down one's life for a spouse, a child, and a world in desperate need of truly heroic people.

People like Mark. He lost his dream job a few months back through no fault of his own. Wrong place at the wrong time. He is considered one of the best in his field, and he wants to relaunch his vision with another company. But doing so would require moving out of state, away from his wife Barbara's family. Barbara is an emotionally fragile soul. Such a drastic change at this stage of her life could throw her into a tailspin. So Mark has decided to take a mundane job in the local market, causing some to think he lacks initiative. Barbara, on the other hand, considers Mark her hero.

People like Candice. She and her husband, Steve, graduated at the top of their class—the best and brightest, most likely to change the world. They tied the knot and launched their partnership. As expected, their combined brains and talents shot them to the top of their field. Each enjoyed a good income and the lifestyle it afforded. Each routinely received accolades for his and her accomplishments. But when they had children, Candice decided to walk away from it all in order to stay home and nurture them. She doesn't question the choice. She does, however, feel a loss. While Steve continues to change the world through the professional pursuits they once chased together, Candice occasionally misses the thrill of success—not to mention the extra income. Her gifts, education, and experience are sitting on a shelf so that she can chase two toddlers around the house and try to keep Cheerios off the floor. She's no longer fulfilling her promise to change the world. Or is she?

Of course, the heroic life goes far beyond marriage and parenting. But it always begins at home.

Many others come to mind because heroes come in all shapes and sizes—from the single mom working two jobs to keep her kids fed, to the underpaid pastor who is overworked and underappreciated caring for the needs of his flock, to the exhausted daughter caring for an aging parent who has forgotten her name. Be it the young man who abandons the freedom of bachelor living to take on the responsibility of a wife and family or the attractive young woman who saves herself for and gives herself to one man for a lifetime, it is in the act of self-sacrifice that we discover the rich beauty and abiding satisfaction that come from a life lived as somebody's hero.

Mini-Tip   CELEBRATING HEROES

When you see a person sacrificing him- or herself for another, take a moment to celebrate such heroic acts with a comment. When you drive by the fire station, tell the kids how thankful you are for those men and women who save lives. When you see a mother or father pushing a baby in a stroller, point out that babies could not survive a week if not for a parent's loving care. When big brother helps little sister into her car seat, ask the family to give him a sitting ovation for his heroic deed. In big and small moments, reinforce for your kids the importance of self-sacrifice in everyday life.

CHAPTER 17

Mini-Saints

ADMIRING COURAGEOUS TIMES

How was he?" asks Kent's mother.

"Oh, we had a few problems. But he was great overall," Kurt responds with forced brightness.

"What kind of problems?" inquires Kent's dad.

"Well, I spent a good portion of the hour chasing him all over the building because he didn't want to stay with the group." I can tell by the look on Kent's dad's face that Kent is going to be in trouble when they get home. Kent can tell, too. He starts apologizing like a drowning man screaming for a rope.

"That's all right, Kent. We'll do better next time." I only half believe it, but it is the thing to say at such a moment.

"Why didn't you come get us out of the service?" asks Mom, the same woman who expressed relief when dropping off her son. She had said that she "really needed to go to church," clearly exhausted from a week of chasing Kent. Like several kids in this class, Kent needs special attention. That's why we call it Special Friends.

We had, in fact, almost called them. Our church has a number system that enables volunteers to summon a child's parent from the main worship service if problems arise. But we remembered his mom's exhausted face and couldn't bring ourselves to interrupt her one-hour break—her one hour of much needed refreshment.

"Listen, don't worry about it." She obviously felt concerned that Kent might be wearing down the volunteers, causing them to abandon the special needs class or ban him from attending altogether. "You deal with his energy all week long. We can manage it for an hour. We didn't want to disturb you."

I don't know if that made her feel any better, but her thanks seemed sincere.

My husband and I periodically help out in various children's classes at church. Our rotation includes the special needs class. Usually only a handful of kids attend, with varying degrees of "special," including autism, mental retardation, physical disabilities, or, like Kent, severe attention deficit hyperactivity disorder. A handful in every sense of the word.

We find something uniquely rewarding about the Special Friends class. Sure, it can get chaotic, even frustrating. But something, well, *special* happens there.

When we walk in we are confident, glad to be heroically filling the most difficult volunteer roles. But by the time we walk out, I feel completely inept. And completely in awe. Waving good-bye to the parents, a lump in my throat, I realize that the true heroes are those worn-down moms and dads who deal with such chaotic frustrations all week, all month, all year.

I become too easily annoyed with my kids when they forget homework or lazily neglect the passing ball during a soccer game. Kent's parents would trade anything for such insignificant irritations. Teenaged Katie sits on the floor next to a toy, rocking back and forth the entire hour. Unlike us, her parents don't worry about how to pay for their daughter's college or wedding expenses. They worry about who will care for her when they become too old.

After church one Sunday my husband spoke to

the Browns, the parents of one particularly difficult special-needs child. Their then-six-year-old daughter, Milly, had been born with a disorder so rare it had not been named. She required continual care and attention. They wondered aloud whether the church might start a program to help such families cope with the unrelenting stress. "It would mean so much to families like ours if we could just get a break now and again." Not that attempts hadn't been made. The typical, well-meaning volunteer came to the house in order to give the Browns a daylong break. Nervous about leaving Milly with someone ill prepared for her outbursts, aggression, and tantrums, they did their best to explain the task at hand.

"Don't worry about it," came the typical reply. "I'm sure we'll be fine."

Six to eight hours later, the Browns came home to an obviously frazzled volunteer, who barely veiled her relief at their arrival. "How was she?" they asked, bracing for the worst.

"Oh, she is such a precious little girl." True. "We had a fine time together!" A bare-faced lie. They knew their daughter had been her usual self and that the volunteer was trying to put a happy face on things. They also presumed they would never see her again. They would be right.

I'm certain the Browns would prefer to hear something like, "Your daughter was a lot of work. What time do you need me next week?" If only people would be real. What helps is someone willing to serve, despite the hard reality—something very few of us have the courage to do.

Most of us feel a bit awkward around those with special needs, at least until we build a relationship. I'm not sure why. It may have something to do with our desire to say or do the right thing without knowing what that right thing is. Do we act as if nothing is wrong so the family feels as though they fit in? Or do we lower our voices and eyes in sympathy for the heartache they endure? The former feels dishonest, the latter condescending.

But our awkward feelings have a much deeper root. Our stomach becomes tense because the disabled know and quietly proclaim the undeniable reality that something is wrong. Seeing them trapped in a difficult experience reminds us that life is unfair. It raises questions with no easy answers. Why are some people healthy, beautiful, and driving red convertibles, while others spend a lifetime needing others to dress them? Why is one child placed in the gifted track, another in special needs? Both sets of parents love their child and long to protect him or her from the hardships and heartaches of life.

But the daily reality of the second quickly drains much hope of success.

During a recent party we found my then four-year-old son Troy hiding in the closet, frightened by a teenaged boy with a deformed face.

"I'm afraid of that guy with the face," he explained.

So we began bringing our boys with us when we volunteer in the Special Friends class—partly to help us but mostly because we want them to push past natural kids' fears of those who are different. We want them to become comfortable relating to the disabled.

I'll admit to subconsciously averting my eyes and walking past a person living with disability. I force myself to smile, greet, or do nothing, depending upon what seems appropriate. But the initial reaction still occurs, as if we are hardwired to avoid feeling awkward. It is like some internal mechanism in our hearts attempts to distract itself from what it knows to be true but wishes were false. And so I—we naturally turn away before willing ourselves back.

Not everyone forces himself back. I remember Kurt sharing a conversation he had with a high-ranking official in then-communist Russia, who was on a lecture tour in the United States. The official agreed to a question-and-answer session in Kurt's office. When asked his first impressions of our society, the Russian made an interesting comment: "I am surprised by your compassion and care for the disabled." He then described our wheelchair ramps, special-access restrooms, reserved parking, and other accommodations for the handicapped. "In Soviet Union, we do not have such things." Apparently, an atheistic society sees no particular reason to accommodate those unable to advance the collective good.

Mother Teresa stuck out like a sore thumb in India precisely because she didn't accept the principle of Karma, a doctrine that serves as the foundation for ethics throughout the Hindu world. Pantheism sees God as everything and everything as God. God is not a person we worship but a force in which we dwell. Karma teaches that those who suffer are paying off a debt from a former life, purifying themselves in this life so that they can reincarnate into something better in the next. The entire caste system depends upon the premise that we are destined to pay in one life for what we did wrongly in a previous life. To help those suffering is to prolong their debt. That is why the sick, poor, and disabled suffer so in Hindu countries.

Their suffering is meant to be. So, in the name of compassion, their religion tells the healthy to avert their eyes.

Those who believe in a personal God, however, force their eyes back. They consider caring for the poor and disabled heroic. Survival of the fittest is a malady to cure, not a reality to accept. God cares for the needy through the heroic, through those willing to sacrifice themselves on behalf of another. But that kind of redemption doesn't come easy. It requires heroes, like the volunteers who help special needs kids for an hour on Sunday. No—like the exhausted parents who love their disabled child for a lifetime.

Mini-Tip SPECIAL NEEDS

Make an intentional effort to create opportunities for your children to interact on a routine basis with special needs children and the elderly in need of care and attention. Since we live in a society that tends to isolate the less than perfect, many children develop unhealthy attitudes or fears of the disabled. Our children need to learn that every human life reflects the image of God and deserves our respect and concern. The best way to learn about them is to befriend and serve them.

CHAPTER 18

Mini-Perfections

ACCEPTING THANKFUL TIMES

Troy sat at the counter, eating a bowl of cereal, a nightly routine for all four of our children. Despite the three-course meal I served only ninety minutes earlier, my kids always feign starvation fifteen minutes before going to bed. I suppose that is why our milk and cereal budget exceeds the house payment.

Anyway, Troy had a look of deep contemplation on his face, milk dripping from the side of his mouth, as he began talking over his half-swallowed mouthful of Rice Krispies.

"I think Daddy is one of the best in the world!"

I noticed Kurt turning to look at his then

seven-year-old fan, not sure whether to relish the praise or question the "one of" qualifier.

"Isn't Daddy the absolute best in the world?" I asked, offering Troy the opportunity to clarify.

"Well," came Troy's less than hoped for reply, "I would score Daddy at 9.1 out of 10."

My eyes met Kurt's. We both wondered the same question, but he beat me to the punch. "Why not score Daddy a ten?"

Troy swallowed hard before replying, "Because nobody's perfect." His grin told us a 9.1 was indeed a compliment to enjoy.

Listening in on the conversation, Nicole decided to add her perspective. No sooner had the words "nobody's perfect" left Troy's lips than Nicole shouted, "Mommy is!"

We had a good laugh, and I secretly relished the affirmation. Reading between the lines and beneath the words, however, I knew what Troy and Nicole were really saying: Daddy is great because he works hard to provide for us, plays ball when we ask, and carries us to bed when we fall asleep in the car. But we prefer Mommy because she smells nice, dresses pretty, and calls us "sweetheart" and "beautiful" instead of "buddy" and "silly filly."

In short, moms have an unfair advantage in

the parental battle of the sexes because we get to reflect the more tender parts of God's image.

About five years before the parental scoring incident, Kurt and I conducted a little activity with the three older boys when they were ages three to eleven. Hoping to help them understand the perfect character of God, we built a scale using a plastic Nerf basketball stand. After securing a shopping bag on each side of the balancing pole, we gave out the instructions.

"You need to look around and find stuff to place in the bags. But, remember, you must put the same amount of weight in each side or the scale will fall over."

Accepting the challenge, they went off to find materials that seemed about the same size and weight to bring back for our experiment. As the oldest, Kyle took charge of the insertion process— careful to ensure equal distribution despite little Troy's desire to indiscriminately throw anything and everything into the bags.

"Well done!" came Kurt's unbiased evaluation. "You have done a great job keeping the two sides in balance."

Next, Kurt took a black marker and wrote a single word on each bag. On the left bag he wrote "justice" and on the right "love." As had been the pattern on family nights, the boys settled in for a brief explanation of the activity.

"You see, our God is a God of perfect justice and perfect love." While Troy wondered when we would get back to throwing stuff in the bags, Kyle and Shaun listened to Dad's explanation of a God of perfect balance.

"I don't know about you," Kurt continued, "but I sometimes wish God was all love. I don't like when He becomes angry at sin or gives us strict rules to obey." The boys could relate. After all, Daddy could be strict at times also. "But what would happen if we got rid of all the stuff in the justice bag?"

Now came Troy's moment as Kurt invited him to remove some of the larger items in the left bag. Immediately, the scale fell over.

"You see, God must be both love and justice or He wouldn't be perfect."

Kurt placed the objects back in the left-hand bag, and returned the scale—and God—to his upright and balanced position.

"Daddy and Mommy are also supposed to balance love and justice in order to represent God and to keep our home from falling over." After inviting the boys to read a few related Scripture passages, we wrapped up our activity and unleashed Troy to destroy our temporary scale.

Later that evening, the boys were sitting at the kitchen counter eating—you guessed it—bowls of cereal. Kyle got an odd look on his face, like he had had an epiphany in response to our scale activity.

"Mom," he began, "I've been thinking."

"About what?" I asked.

"About you and Dad. I think Dad is seventy-five percent justice and twenty-five percent love. But I think you are seventy-five percent love and only twenty-five percent justice."

A smile came across my face. Kyle had nailed our basic natures and parenting styles. Together, we created a pretty good reflection of our heavenly Father. But neither Mom nor Dad had perfect balance. Mom's scale tips a bit too much toward words associated with love—like *nurture* and *affirmation*. Dad's scale tips a bit too much toward words associated with justice—like *discipline* and *strength*.

It just so happens, kids tend to grade justice at 9.1 while they give love a 10. I know it isn't fair, and it certainly isn't balanced. But, since someone has to be the favorite, it might as well be us girls.

When our children are very young—ages one through three—we imprint their lives by how we treat them rather than by instructional activities. It is in this season that we impress their hearts, not their heads. Because children form their early view of God largely from how they view their parents, we can use the early years to reinforce the character of God—including both His love and His justice. And the best way for a mom to impress the love of God upon their hearts is by doing what comes naturally. We should overwhelm them with affirmation and affection—including lots of hugs and kisses—and praise for their fledgling attempts to talk, walk, and feed themselves. In these small ways, we are demonstrating unconditional love and the kind of affection God has for us. (By the way, don't stop as the child ages!)

In addition to establishing the security of unconditional love and affection when our children are very young, it is important to establish a clear sense that Mom and Dad set the rules and the child is expected to obey those rules. Starting when your child is about eighteen months old, you should establish some consistent system of discipline when your child willfully defies your rules. We demonstrate God's character when we refuse to tolerate rebellion against the rules we've established. Please note, however, that there is a difference between willful defiance and childish irresponsibility. Like God, we must clarify right from wrong with children and bring about appropriate discipline when violated. Parents who neglect this principle during the early years risk giving children the mistaken idea that love and justice are mutually exclusive. God is both, and we must try to model both. Some excellent resources to help you implement this balance include *Dare to Discipline* and *Hide or Seek*, both written by Dr. James Dobson.

Mini-Tip   PERSONALITY CHECK

Every husband-and-wife duo is unique. Take one of the many personality tests together to figure out which tends to be more fun and playful and which tends to be more structured and strict. (One of the most fun personality tests is found in Dr. John Trent's book *The Language of Love* available from www.strongfamilies.com.) Then create a game plan for making sure you leverage both strengths to avoid one extreme or the other in your home. In our home, this exercise has been helpful in keeping my husband from always having to play disciplinarian because I want to remain the life of the party.

CHAPTER 19

Mini-Losses

GRIEVING-DYING TIMES

Her silence said everything. Already we sensed that something must be wrong. That's why we made an appointment.

During my fifth month of pregnancy, I should have felt the baby kicking, so that I could have excitedly pulled Kurt's hand onto my belly for him to feel it, too. The baby seemed healthy weeks earlier—a strong heartbeat prompting the usual excitement. When that changed, we became anxious, called the doctor, and obediently visited the radiology lab. The technician spread the gel and moved the ultrasound probe around my abdomen, as she did during Kyle and Shaun's stay in the womb. We saw faint images on the screen that looked like a head and an arm, just as before. But this time was different. I noticed the technician staring at the screen and making notes as if trying to avoid eye contact. She hates this part of her job.

We drove to the doctor's office to learn the results. Only doctors are allowed to deliver bad news. During the trip we didn't speak, both of us feeling the dread of imminent grief. "I'm sorry about your baby." The doctor's warm, compassionate voice opened the dike of tears. As we had guessed, our baby had died.

The next several hours were among the most traumatic of our lives. I checked into the hospital; then endured five hours of induced labor and delivered a child who would never breathe. The nurses sensitively put us in a room down the hall, away from the maternity ward. The last thing we needed to hear was the happy sound of crying newborns. The hospital reserved our hall for another kind of crying.

Kurt managed to remain strong until shortly after the delivery of the stillborn baby. Our friends arrived at the hospital with our older boys. Kyle was then five, old enough to feel very excited about baby Todd's impending arrival but too young to understand the loss. Kurt had the task of trying to explain to him something he didn't understand himself.

"The baby died," Kurt said in a trembling voice.

Kyle's eyes immediately filled with tears. "Why?" came the question with no answer. Just a few days earlier, Kyle had been making plans to play with his new sibling. Now, he was fumbling to fit the square peg of death into the round hole of life.

I suppose Kurt could have said something about God taking Todd so that He could have another baby in heaven or death being a natural part of life. But he didn't. Todd had simply died—it happens. And it is sad. So Kurt explained that we had to love Mommy and cry together, which we did in the quiet hospital wing, now dark with sorrow.

We had encountered death before. My beloved grandma died when I was fairly young—but grandmas are supposed to die. My absentee, alcoholic father died during my senior year of high school. But we weren't close, and I grieved less than I probably should have. Kurt's best boyhood friend, Don, had been killed in a plane crash at age twenty-one, leaving a young wife and baby behind. And then there was Cheryl, Kurt's thirty-something aunt, who was like a second mom to him. She knew the cancer would take her, so she asked Kurt and me to sing at her funeral. One of her favorite songs was

"Someday You'll Never Have to Say Good-Bye." But we *were* saying good-bye. We wept more than we sang. Thirty-something is too young to die. So is twenty-one. So is the fifth month.

Fast-forward five years. Kurt bounced out the doors of that same hospital, this time joyously leaving the maternity ward heading to our car in the parking lot to pick up Kyle, Shaun, and three-year-old Troy so that they could see Mommy and their new little sister.

Skipping toward our car, Kurt noticed an acquaintance walking in the other direction, heading into the hospital. Remembering the man's wife had been pregnant, Kurt flashed a big smile. "We just had a girl!" He couldn't contain himself. "How about you?"

It was not good news. The couple had lost their baby, the little boy desperately wanted after having a girl. Kurt recognized the pain in the man's voice from our own journey through grief over Todd. He said something about understanding what they were going through. The man gave a faint nod of appreciation before turning down the hall, away from the maternity ward.

It seems strange, but fitting, that our round hole of new life would encounter death's square peg, forcing its way into another home. Sad for our friend but glad our grief had passed, we knew that it will surely strike our home again. It might take a friend, a parent, a spouse, or our precious little girl. It will probably come unexpectedly, perhaps cruelly, certainly unwelcome. And no matter how hard we try to be strong or try to accept death as natural, we will cry.

A child gets struck down by a drunk driver. Another starves in a war-torn third-world nation, while a third is aborted before given a shot at life.

A woman suffers the cruel deterioration of Alzheimer's disease. Another passes away peacefully in her sleep, while a third suffocates next to her daughter in a Nazi gas chamber.

A man hacks and coughs his lungs out from cancer caused by a lifetime of smoking. Another wastes away in a nursing home, while a third dies falling from a ladder in a freak accident.

No matter how it happens, we never welcome death. So we try to avoid its terror by pretending—avoiding its truth with lies. We replace tearful silence with well-intentioned but idiotic pep talks. Humble resignation gets drowned out by defiance, denial, or blame.

Finally, in a last-ditch effort to fend off terror, we concoct the final lie: "Even when death comes, it is nothing to fear. Like childbirth, it is a natural part of life's cycle."

Of course, deep down, we know better.

I believe that grief and fear are proper responses precisely because death is *unnatural*. God is the source of life. So life reflects His nature—natural. Death doesn't—unnatural. Certainly, everyone dies. But the fact that something bad happens to everyone doesn't make it good. And we never become more aware of what's wrong than when we grieve over a loved one's death—or fear our own. Like a hand reacting to a match's flame, our lives rightfully flinch at death's assault.

When we went to the nursing home to pick up my mom while she was alive, we walked down a hall one would avoid if possible. Most of the residents there looked to be in the final stages of life—or the early stages of death. Only the electronic glow and competing sounds of sitcoms, game shows, and weather reports infused any illusion of activity. We felt, based upon some people's reactions there to our noisy children, that the sound of young life seemed unwelcome in this wing, much like in the one down the hall from the maternity ward. The last thing those in death's waiting room want to hear is children. Their hall is reserved for another kind of crying: the chronic, lonely sorrow of a lie that steals

the compassion they deserve. Friends and family ig-
nore most of them. Those who do visit shout silly
pep talks about their looking good and the fun of
craft class, as if nothing were seriously wrong.

But something is wrong. It is something we fear
and something we grieve. As well we should.

I grieved over the loss of baby Todd, the child I
never held in my arms.

I grieved over the death of my mother, the
woman who once held me in hers.

Someday, I will grieve over other losses—pos-
sibly my husband, a dear friend, or even one of
my precious children. If not, then they will grieve
over me. One way or the other, we will encounter
death. And the tears that flow will testify to the
wonderful reality that we were made for life.

Not long after losing Todd, I gave birth to Troy.
A few years later, Nicole arrived. We gave her the
middle name Joy as a fitting reminder of what new
life brings to a family.

Some look at our clan as we get out of our minivan and marvel at such a large family. In an age
when the average woman has only one child, I understand the reaction. And, yes, it is a lot of work.
Every child brings his own demands and challenges.
Every mother, whether they have one child or ten,
knows the kind of sacrifice parenting requires.

In fact, it demands a different type of death. The sort described in Paul's letter to the Philippians.

> Let this mind be in you which was also in Christ Jesus, who . . . made Himself of no reputation, taking the form of a bondservant. . . . He humbled Himself and became obedient to the point of death, even the death of the cross.
>
> PHILIPPIANS 2:5–8, NKJV

We, like Christ, have been called to lay aside concern for reputation, become a servant, humble ourselves, and become obedient—even to the point of death. So, in what I consider one of the great ironies of motherhood, we are called to die to ourselves in order to give life to others. Be it one child, four, or a dozen—motherhood gives us the opportunity to redeem the tears of death by bringing and nurturing life.

Throughout most of history a woman often risked her life giving birth—infusing great relevance to Christ's example. But even those of us who delivered children in the relative safety of a modern hospital are called to lay our lives down on a daily basis that through our "death" they might be given life.

Paul goes on to explain that, after Christ humbled and sacrificed himself for us, God "has highly exalted Him and given Him the name which is above every name."

He does the same for you and me. Our willingness to "die" on behalf of our children earns us the right to wear a title above nearly every other. The life-giving name "mommy."

Mini-Tip   DEATH TO SELF

Set aside some time in the coming week to meditate on Philippians chapter 2. Offer your life to God as one willing to follow Christ's example of dying to self in order to give life to your family and others through service and sacrifice. Memorize the chapter in order to maintain a biblical perspective on motherhood—remembering that you have been called to love your family more than yourself.

Conclusion

For several years our family played a little game that my husband invented to occupy time and keep the kids from picking on one another during minivan drives. Kurt shouted a question about which family member possessed the most of a given characteristic. The kids then raced to shout a response, with an unspoken expectation that everyone would answer in unison. It went like this:

KURT: Who's the tallest?
CHILDREN: Dad is!

Until recently, Dad had that one in the bag. But our oldest recently passed him by about an inch;

coincidentally, the question no longer is asked. Other questions, however, are still in play.

KURT: Who's the hockey-est?
CHILDREN: Troy is!

Although *hockey-est* is not an actual word, they got the point. Troy is a sports nut and star of his hockey team.

KURT: Who's the inventor?
CHILDREN: Shaun is!

Our second son has been coming up with inventions for everything from military weapons to high-tech gadgets since he was tiny. So he always won that one.

DAD: Who's the prettiest?
CHILDREN: Mom is!

I had no problem winning that one until Nicole came along, forcing Kurt to create a new category.

DAD: Who's the princess?
CHILDREN: Nicole is!

For the longest time we enjoyed this little game together, covering every imaginable characteristic the members of our family possessed. At least every imaginable positive characteristic, since the intent was to reinforce a healthy sense of identity and affirm how God uniquely gifted each member of the family. That's why it surprised me the time Kurt shouted a characteristic that seemed to violate the game's objective.

DAD: Who's the smartest?

Caught off guard, I turned to look at Kurt. He figured the kids would immediately shout, "Dad is!"

A split second later, our then six-year-old shouted a different response.

SHAUN: Mom is!

With a gigantic smile on my face, I peered out the corner of my eye at Kurt. He looked deeply hurt. Concealing his wounded pride while clearing his throat, Kurt looked at Shaun in the rearview mirror and asked. "Shaun, I agree that Mommy is smart. I mean, she graduated from college and was a schoolteacher and all. But I have to ask, why did you immediately say Mommy is the smartest?"

"Because," Shaun proclaimed without hesitation, "she always knows when I have to go to the bathroom!"

My self-assured grin dropped as Kurt's frown turned into a smile. I knew what he was thinking: *Well, at least Dad is still smartest when it comes to the important stuff!*

If "the important stuff" is so important, why didn't it show up at the top of Shaun's list? He didn't mention Kurt's graduate degree, stack of sophisticated books he's written, or ability to calculate gas mileage on long trips. But then, neither did Shaun care about my college diploma, elementary education certificate, or ability to teach piano lessons. From Shaun's vantage point, the only thing that really matters is that Mom knows and responds to his needs. And that makes me the undisputed smartest!

What would happen if we gave mothers their due recognition? In academia, those who invest the years of sacrifice and discipline necessary to master a given academic field receive letters to follow their names. Kurt, for example, has an M.A. in theology because he invested three years beyond undergraduate school studying apologetics, church history, Greek, epistemology, and the rest. Our good friend Doug invested a decade of his life earning a Ph.D. in philosophy from the University of Southern California. When Doug finished his dissertation, he could rightfully claim to be the world's foremost authority on his specific topic. Hence, they call him Dr. Gievett.

Contrary to an increasingly common perception, those who hit the pause button on their careers to bear and raise children are not wasting their educations. Nor are they demonstrating a lack of intelligence, ability, or initiative. Like Dr. Gievett, they have committed themselves to dedicate the time and discipline needed to become the world's foremost authority on one or more specific topics. By having my four children I enrolled myself in a very long, arduous curriculum. To earn any letters behind my name I would first need to earn a quadruple major by becoming the smartest person on the planet in the disciplines titled Kyle, Shaun, Troy, and Nicole. Unlike theology, philosophy, physics, mathematics, biology, economics, or any other field of knowledge, however, my field has no formal textbooks or academic adviser to guide me along the way. It is the most challenging form of higher education; 100 percent self-directed study. No sitting in class listening to a professor lecture.

No skimming textbooks for the right answer before a quiz. Just me staring into a microscope to discover the wonder and majesty of four creative masterpieces.

So why shouldn't I have letters behind my name, indicating a level of academic proficiency motherhood deserves? After all, years can pass in which nobody asks Kurt what he knows about the Arian Controversy. I'm certain months go by before Doug is called upon to explain the difference between an ontological and teleological argument. But not a day passes that I don't help the kids make it to the toilet on time.

Who wants a Ph.D. when you can have A.K.A. MOM behind your name?

DAD: Who's the smartest?

Well, when it comes to the really important stuff, Mom is.

My husband and I helped cofound a ministry called the Heritage Builders Association, in part to help those, like me, who hope to give something better to their children than they may have received themselves. We try to help parents understand the multigenerational cycle taking place in every home.

By way of definition, a *heritage* is the emotional, spiritual, and relational legacy that is passed from parent to child . . . good or bad. We all receive one. We all give one. The question is whether we are being intentional about keeping and passing the good we received and strengthening or replacing the bad in order to give something better to our children.

As one who did not have her spiritual, emotional, or social needs met at home, I can't express strongly enough how important little things can be in the formation of a child's security, confidence, and character. But doing the little things to meet my children's spiritual, emotional, and social needs takes intentional effort. It wasn't modeled by my parents for me when I was a child, so it doesn't come naturally to me today. In essence, I am trying to give something I never received. But, as J. Otis Ledbetter shares in his book titled *Your Heritage*, that is precisely the point:

> It just doesn't seem fair, does it? Some were given a wonderful, healthy, positive heritage—a beautiful gown. Others were handed rags. There are people for whom the process of passing a solid heritage is a natural outgrowth of who they

are. Others can't even fathom the experience of positive family living. The good news is that anyone can give a positive heritage. The bad news is that the process of doing so will be much harder for some than others.

You can give what you didn't get. But doing so requires a choice. You can elect to remain a passive victim to your past, or move on to a bright future. The former requires less effort, but more pain. The latter is hard work, but reaps great long-term rewards, for you and for future generations.*

Perhaps you are a mom trying to make the sacrifices necessary to meet the spiritual, emotional, and social needs of your children without the benefit of having had them met for you. Maybe you, like I, wonder whether it is worth the effort. Does anyone even notice? Does anyone have any idea how difficult and thankless it can be trying to meet everyone else's needs all the time?

In truth, people probably have no idea. And they likely don't notice. Which is why I wrote this book.

---

*J. Otis Ledbetter and Kurt Bruner, *Your Heritage* (Colorado Springs: Cook Communications Ministries, 1999), p. 183.

I want to celebrate the hectic joys of motherhood. Hectic because they are rarely planned and often uninvited. Joys because they are always meaningful, even when obtained through the sheer grit of serving the needs of my children when I'd rather be shopping, napping, or actually finishing the cup of tea I intended to drink when I sat in front of the fireplace to read a good book. I want moms to take a few moments to reflect upon just how important they are and just how much joy they can derive from little moments—milking all the encouragement possible from a child, who can consider every person he or she knows on the planet and without hesitation unwittingly crown Mom "the smartest."

ABOUT THE AUTHOR

Olivia Bruner and her husband are in the middle of "the minivan years" with their own four children. As a featured author and speaker for the Heritage Builders Association, she inspires parents to celebrate the hectic joys of parenting and become intentional about giving a strong heritage to the next generation. A former sixth grade teacher, Olivia is a popular speaker for parents and educators and has been a frequent guest on the Focus on the Family broadcast. To learn more about Olivia, visit www.oliviabruner.com.